THE
DAY
JFK
DIED

THE DAY JFK DIED

Thirty years later:
The event that
changed a generation

The Dallas Morning News

ANDREWS AND McMEEL
A Universal Press Syndicate Company
KANSAS CITY

The Dallas Morning News

Publisher and Editor

Burl Osborne

Senior Vice President and Executive Editor

Ralph Langer

All of the text and some of the photographs in this book originally appeared as a special commemorative section of *The Dallas Morning News* on November 20, 1988.

The editors wish to thank the following, who provided photographs for this book:

The Bettmann Archive
The Dallas Morning News
Bob Jackson
LMH Company
National Archives and
 Records Administration
Wide World Photos

Some of the photographs in this book still carry the retouching marks from earlier publication.

It has been thirty years since the assassination of President John F. Kennedy shocked the world and forever etched itself into the shared memory of the United States. This book by the staff of *The Dallas Morning News* is a retrospective chronicle in words and pictures of a tragic and fateful period in our history.

Burl Osborne

President and Editor
The Dallas Morning News

Library of Congress Cataloging-in-Publication Data

The Day JFK died : thirty years later : the event that changed a generation / The Dallas morning news.

    p.   cm.
   ISBN: 0-8362-6247-6
   1. Kennedy, John F. (John Fitzgerald), 1917 – 1963 — Assassination.
 I. Dallas morning news.

E842.9.D3   1993
973.922′092 — dc20   93-21170
                                          CIP

CONTENTS

President John F. Kennedy addresses a large crowd in Fort Worth, Texas, early on the morning of November 22, 1963.

THE TENOR OF THE TIMES

Far-right-wingers and Democratic Discord Set the Stage for Kennedy's Visit

by Steve Blow and Sam Attlesey

Though seldom calm, the political atmosphere was supercharged in Texas in the autumn of 1963.

Among the Democrats, top leaders were engaged in a bitter feud. Among the Republicans, conservatives were in control and the ultraconservative fringe appeared to be out of control.

Yet there was hope for easing tensions on all sides through a single event — the impending visit to Texas of President John F. Kennedy.

City leaders saw the visit as a chance to erase the embarrassment caused by two nationally publicized incidents involving far-right Republicans. Democrats, meanwhile, saw a number of possible benefits from the trip.

Most Texas politicians said the president planned his visit to shore up support for his upcoming 1964 election campaign and to pry loose some of the Texas wealth for his political coffers.

But Kennedy associates said the trip was to heal the increasingly nasty personal and philosophical rift among three of the most powerful Texas Democrats — Vice President Lyndon B. Johnson, Gov. John Connally and U.S. Sen. Ralph Yarborough.

"The president was trying to get the political situation settled in Texas," Attorney General Robert Kennedy said later in an interview.

"I know that was the point of the trip, to heal everything, to get everybody to ride in the same car or something," Jacqueline Kennedy recalled.

The usual struggle between the liberal and conservative wings of the Texas Democratic Party had been compounded by the conflicts among the three powerful and ambitious main characters in the Democratic drama.

Johnson, the master politician who had ruled the Senate for years, was painfully adjusting to the secondary role of vice president.

Conservative Connally, the pin-striped rancher who had gained much of his political acumen from Johnson, was rapidly becoming a favorite of the state's business community.

Liberal Yarborough, the East Texas populist lawyer, had angered Johnson when he supported Kennedy for the 1960 presidential nomination instead of fellow Texan Johnson.

All three of the strong-willed Texans were up for re-election in 1964, and Yarborough was convinced that Johnson and Connally were plotting to find a candidate to unseat him.

To further muddy the water, rumors swirled that Kennedy was being urged to dump Johnson from the ticket in 1964. On the day before Kennedy arrived in Dallas, his former opponent, Richard Nixon, visited the city and predicted that Kennedy would replace Johnson.

The president's four-day Texas visit did not begin well. In San Antonio and again in Houston, Yarborough refused to ride with Johnson in the presidential motorcade. The two did, however, share a stage with Kennedy in Fort Worth early on the morning of Nov. 22.

And Kennedy had prepared a speech of political reconciliation to be delivered that night at a fund-raising dinner in Austin. It was to be the finale of the Texas trip. "So let us not be petty when our cause is so great," the speech read. "Let us not quarrel amongst ourselves when our nation's future is at stake."

But before making that speech in Austin, Kennedy was to visit Dallas, where there was a very different brand of political tumult afoot.

The Republican Party had surged to life in Dallas County in the late 1950s. In 1960, Dallas gave Nixon the largest vote margin over Kennedy of any city in the country. In elections over the next three years, eight of Dallas County's nine state Legislature seats went Republican.

But while mainstream conservatives dominated the politics, extremist conservatives dominated the political image of the city. Dallas was considered a major center of a fiery far-right movement that was sweeping the nation.

In the aftermath of the assassination, two previous incidents involving the extremists came to symbolize the so-called "climate of hate" in Dallas.

The first incident occurred in November 1960 — four days before the presidential election — when vice presidential candidate Johnson encountered a throng of Nixon supporters on a downtown street.

In October 1963, U.N. Ambassador Adlai Stevenson is struck by a sign carried by a woman picketer (right) at Dallas' Memorial Auditorium.

As Johnson and his wife, Lady Bird, prepared to walk across Commerce Street from the Baker Hotel to a luncheon at the Adolphus Hotel, they were confronted by several hundred jeering, placard-waving protesters. One carried a Johnson campaign poster with "Smiling Judas" scrawled next to Johnson's photo. Another placard borrowed from a then-current lingerie advertisement: "He Dreamed He Went to Washington in His Turncoat."

Among those at the front of the mob, shouting at Johnson and carrying a placard that read "LBJ Sold Out to the Yankee Socialists," was Dallas congressman Bruce Alger — the only Texas Republican in Congress at the time.

Security officers suggested that Johnson use side doors to avoid the crowd, but Johnson refused. "No, I only hope

the day never comes when a man cannot walk his lady across the street in Dallas," Johnson said.

He and Mrs. Johnson did manage to cross the street, but it took 45 minutes as the taunting mob jostled them from all sides. Mrs. Johnson's hair was mussed, and Johnson later said that they were spat upon.

In those last days of the campaign, the Dallas incident became one of Johnson's primary topics. Discussing the demonstrators while campaigning in Houston, Johnson even invoked Jesus' words on the cross: "God, forgive them, for they know not what they do."

The second incident that shaped Dallas' political image across the nation occurred almost three years later — less than a month before Kennedy's visit.

On Oct. 24, 1963, U.N. Ambassador Adlai Stevenson visited Dallas to speak at a U.N. Day program at Memorial Auditorium, now known as the Dallas Convention Center arena.

Among the 2,000 people attending that night were about 100 right-wing extremists who intended to show their disdain for the United Nations. At the time, a motto of the far right often seen on billboards and bumper stickers was "Get the U.S. Out of the U.N. and the U.N. Out of the U.S."

During Stevenson's speech, the protesters coughed in cadence and walked the aisles carrying U.S. flags upside down as a sign of distress. At one point, Frank McGehee, leader of the Dallas-based National Indignation Committee, stood and began shouting. Stevenson brushed him off with a quip as police escorted McGehee out of the auditorium.

Wes Wise, who later would become mayor of Dallas, was there that night as a reporter for television station KRLD, now KDFW (Channel 4). "There was an electric atmosphere in that place," Wise said later. "I wouldn't exactly call it an atmosphere of hate, but there was an atmosphere."

Although his deadline for the 10 p.m. newscast was nearing, Wise decided to stay at the auditorium in case there was trouble after Stevenson's speech. His instincts proved sound.

As Stevenson was walking from the auditorium, a woman swung her anti-U.N. placard and struck him on the head. Wise was close behind with his camera rolling. A newspaper photographer also recorded the moment. The woman, an Oak Cliff homemaker, later said she had accidentally hit Stevenson when she was bumped by someone in the crowd.

To cap off the evening, as Dallas retailer Stanley Marcus escorted the stunned ambassador to a waiting car, an Irving college student spat on Stevenson. "There was a mob scene that night," Marcus recalled. "After I shoved him in the car, they (the protesters) started rocking the car, and the driver had to gun the car and almost kill a person to get out."

The incident made national news. Wise's film was shown in slow motion by Walter Cronkite on CBS News the next evening, and newspapers published the photo on their front pages.

Clearly, the extremists were not as harmless as Dallas leaders had assumed them to be. But neither were they as powerful as the world assumed them to be after the assassination.

Many Dallas leaders agree with the Warren Commission finding that the assassination was unrelated to the political turmoil in Dallas at the time.

"It was a coincidence. It just happened in a place where the pot was boiling," said the late Willis Tate, who was president of Southern Methodist University at the time. As SMU president,

Tate got a firsthand view of the actions of the ultraconservatives. He was bombarded with community protest when left-leaning speakers appeared on campus. Right-wingers, according to newspaper reports, began referring to SMU as "the Kremlin on the hill."

"The pot was boiling because people were frightened. These people were all scared. I didn't understand it — I lived through it, but I didn't understand it," said Tate, who won the American Association of University Professors' Meiklejohn Award for supporting academic freedom during the period.

James Brown, a political science professor at SMU, has a file folder bulging with right-wing fliers he collected in Dallas during the early '60s. Some portrayed Johnson as an ally of the Communists. Many called for the impeachment of U.S. Supreme Court Chief Justice Earl Warren.

"This gives you the tenor of the times," Brown said. "People were running around professing to protect the democratic process but using totalitarian tactics to achieve their goals. In many ways, they were no better than fascists."

The rhetoric of the right was powerful. At the first National Indignation Convention in Dallas in November 1961, ultraconservative Texan J. Evetts Haley laughingly said impeachment of Warren wasn't good enough. Haley called for a hanging.

Dallas also gained some attention as the home of billionaire oilman H.L. Hunt, who often was featured in magazine articles of that time as the world's richest man. The articles noted his ultraconservatism, which he sought to spread through the *Facts Forum* and *Lifeline* national radio programs.

After the assassination, Dallas frequently was referred to as the capital of the far right, although news accounts of the ultraconservative movement had never made such a case before November 1963. Even at the height of their activity in Dallas, the right-wing extremists were a small group. But they managed to draw big attention.

"These people were fairly well-funded," Brown said. "Many came from the middle class. They were educated. They were articulate. They knew how to use public opinion and public relations."

Looking back on that time, Marcus said, "I believe that there was a spirit of hate that existed in Dallas — in the strong Republican districts in North Dallas where people believe they had the only true and revealed truth and could not conceive of any pluralism in society."

"And they were aided and abetted by the newspaper," Marcus said. "*The Dallas News* was the one instrument that could have refuted that point of view, but it didn't. It just aided and abetted it."

At that time, the editorial page of *The Dallas Morning News* had gained a national reputation among journalists and politicians for its unswervingly conservative and often acerbic viewpoints. An editorial columnist referred to the New Deal as the "Queer Deal," to the American Civil Liberties Union as the "American Swivel Liberties Union" and to the U.S. Supreme Court as the "Judicial Kremlin."

Marcus and other critics accused *The News'* editorial page of polarizing the issues and of encouraging the far right's stridency and disrespect for national institutions.

Dick West, editorial director of the newspaper at the time, said years later, "I don't know whether it encouraged disrespect or not. But many, many people applauded what we were saying."

If Dallas was different from other cities at the time, it was in the degree of acceptance that the far right enjoyed. There are differing opinions, however, on the level of that acceptance.

Some Dallas leaders say the extremists were simply ignored because they were such an insignificant group. "It was just a handful of little people — not representative of the community at all," the late C.A. Tatum Jr., who was president of the Dallas Citizens Council in 1961, said in a 1983 interview.

Conservative politicians say the extremists represented a minority viewpoint that never infiltrated mainstream conservatism. But leaders of the time clearly had to walk a fine line to appease both groups. "There were some problems in those days," said John Tower, who was elected in 1961 as the first Republican U.S. senator from the South since Reconstruction. "But I got along with everybody. I never chastised anyone or read the riot act to anyone." Tower died in a plane crash in April 1991.

Some say the extremist viewpoint wasn't just tolerated in Dallas but was quietly embraced. "The old boys (establishment leaders) sympathized with these folks," said Bruce Pringle, a sociologist at SMU at the time, now retired in Seattle. "They didn't like violence and all that, but they could certainly see what all the hollering was about."

Dallas lawyer Sid Stahl, who later served on the City Council, watched the actions of the far right from a vantage point as vice chairman of the Jewish Federation's Community Relations Council. He didn't like what he was seeing.

"They seemed to be receiving more and more prominence and attracting more and more of the respectable groups of citizens in the community. It was scary," he said.

In the wake of the Stevenson incident, Dallas leaders realized that the ultraconservatives were out of control. "These are not conservatives — they are radicals," then-Dallas Mayor Earle Cabell said in a harsh rebuke.

Dallas was embarrassed and repentant over humiliating Stevenson. *The Dallas Morning News* published an editorial extending a "community apology" to Stevenson, assuring him that "the actions of a few do not represent the demeanor of the rest." *The Dallas Times Herald* published a front-page editorial headlined "Dallas Disgrace."

Telegrams signed by 100 civic leaders were sent to Kennedy and Stevenson saying that Dallas was "outraged and abjectly ashamed" of the incident. The City Council quickly passed an anti-harassment ordinance.

In a statement issued two days after the October 1963 incident, Cabell said civic leaders must accept some responsibility for the problem in Dallas. "The constructive thinker and civic builder, although in the majority, has become engrossed in his own affairs and has permitted a small but highly vocal minority to project the image of our city to the world at large."

But Cabell also saw a way for the city to clear its name. "We have an opportunity to redeem ourselves," he said, "when the president pays us a visit next month."

This article, written for The News' *1983 special report on the Kennedy assassination, was updated in 1988 and in 1993.*

IN THEIR OWN WORDS

November 22–25, 1963

John Fitzgerald Kennedy arose Friday, Nov. 22, 1963, in a Fort Worth hotel. Three days later, he was buried in Arlington National Cemetery.

This is the story of those four days, in the words of the people who were there. The recollections come from interviews by The Dallas Morning News *in 1983 and 1988, and from documents at the John F. Kennedy and Lyndon B. Johnson libraries and other archives. Those quoted are identified by the titles they held at the time of the assassination.*

All times given are Dallas time.

NOV. 22

FRIDAY

7 a.m.

Evelyn Lincoln, President Kennedy's personal secretary, begins her day in the Hotel Texas in Fort Worth with a brief visit to the president.

Mrs. Lincoln: "I dressed in a dark blue suit and then asked a maid to clean the room. I had some friends from Dallas coming to have breakfast.

"I walked to the president's room… and asked him if he'd mind meeting my friends.

"He told the Secret Service to let me know when he started to leave so I could bring my friends out to the hallway to meet him.…He was in a very happy mood."

7:10 a.m.

Lee Harvey Oswald knocks on the front door of the Irving home of Wesley Frazier, an order clerk at the Texas School Book Depository in downtown Dallas, where both work. Oswald sometimes rides to work with Frazier.

Frazier: "He came down…as I was eating my breakfast.…I left for work a few minutes after 7.

"And when I came out to get into the car, I glanced over and saw a package in the back seat. I said, 'What's that?' and he said, 'You remember — that's the curtain rods I was going to bring in.'

"It was kind of a misting rain.…Everybody knew by that time that President Kennedy was coming to Dallas and he was coming down (past the book depository) on the parade route.

"As we rode to work that morning, we talked about it. I said it may not be a good day for a parade."

The Dallas Morning News

Accompanied by (from left) Sen. Yarborough and Rep. Jim Wright, President Kennedy crosses the street in front of the Hotel Texas in Fort Worth.

The Dallas Morning News

First lady Jacqueline Kennedy chats with Vice President and Mrs. Johnson during a breakfast at the Hotel Texas. The president is at the far right.

7:30 a.m.

Peter Saccu, catering manager of the Hotel Texas, oversees preparation of Kennedy's breakfast. Jacqueline Kennedy will eat later.

Saccu: "The president had soft-boiled eggs, bacon, dry toast with marmalade, orange juice and coffee. He had a pretty standard breakfast — very light.

"We were told that he wasn't hard to please — just to make sure his eggs and his coffee were hot."

7:56 a.m.

Frazier and Oswald arrive at the book depository.

Shortly before 8:30 a.m.

Kennedy and Larry O'Brien, a close friend and aide, are at the hotel looking out a window toward the parking lot where the president will give a brief address minutes later.

O'Brien: "They were putting the final touches on the stand out in a large parking lot in front of the hotel where he was going to make an appearance, and he made a comment that 'if someone wanted to get you, it wouldn't be very difficult, would it?'"

8:30 a.m.

Marjorie Belew, wife of Fort Worth lawyer David O. Belew Jr. and Mrs. Kennedy's escort

The Dallas Morning News

Sharing the platform with President Kennedy in front of the Texas Hotel are (from left, foreground) Texas State Sen. Don Kennard, Sen. Ralph Yarborough, Gov. John Connally and Vice President Lyndon Johnson.

to the speech, goes with U.S. Rep. Jim Wright to the Kennedys' hotel suite.

Mrs. Belew: "Mr. Kennedy came out and apologized to me because she wasn't ready, that she had to do something with her hair, but that I would understand — and we would understand if he didn't invite us in.

"I think I was chosen (to escort the Kennedys) because of my ability to make conversation. But I flunked.

"I just stared at him and couldn't think of anything to say. But he was so charming. And finally, I think Congressman Wright said, 'Say something, Marge.' And the president just laughed."

About 8:40 a.m.

Kennedy emerges from his suite again and stops in the hall to greet his secretary's friends.

Mrs. Lincoln: "He gave the usual pleasantries. He said he was pleased to meet them and that any friends of mine were friends of his. He then looked out of the window and commented about how many people were down below. The size of the crowd pleased him."

8:45 a.m.

Mrs. Belew accompanies the president and others in the entourage to the platform for

his speech. Also there are Vice President Lyndon B. Johnson, Sen. Ralph W. Yarborough and Gov. John Connally.

Mrs. Belew: "It was drizzling until we got on the platform and he got up to speak. The sun came out. It was amazing."

Many in the crowd of 5,000 chant: "Where's Jackie? Where's Jackie?" The president points toward the hotel suite. Liz Carpenter, executive assistant to Johnson, stands nearby as the president begins his speech.

Ms. Carpenter: "He realized that the crowd had really wanted to see Mrs. Kennedy, too, and it was very disappointed when she didn't show up.

(Kennedy said) that Mrs. Kennedy had been getting dressed and it takes women longer, but of course, 'Mrs. Kennedy looks better.'"

Shortly before 9 a.m.

Kennedy finishes his brief speech and makes his way through the crowd, shaking hands. As he walks back toward the hotel for a Fort Worth Chamber of Commerce breakfast, he chats with Tarrant County Sheriff Lon Evans.

Evans: "I had my sheriff's posse there to assist with the crowd. So when we came back across the street to the hotel, he asked me, 'Sheriff,' he said, 'are these men Texas Rangers?'"

"I said, 'No, Mr. President, these are members of my sheriff's posse.' He said, 'Would you be kind enough to introduce me to a couple of them?' So I introduced him to a couple of the men on horseback. He was very interested in the horses....He commented on the men's uniforms and everything, which were Western."

The president stops to chat with Mary Ann Glicksman, a 16-year-old junior at R.L. Paschal High School in Fort Worth.

Miss Glicksman: "He was shaking hands with the people in the front row. When he got to me, he stopped and said, 'Aren't you supposed to be in school right now?' I said, 'Well, yes, as a matter of fact, I'm supposed to be taking a test right now.'

"He said, 'You tell your teacher that the president of the United States excused you.'"

9 a.m.

H. Richard Gwozdz, an 8-year-old member of the Texas Boys Choir, is among those who sing a selection of Texas ballads as Kennedy enters the hotel ballroom for the breakfast.

Gwozdz: "He shook the hands of a couple people. I didn't get to. I was too short. I was in the front row, but the platform was in the way and there were other people in front."

9:20 a.m.

Ms. Carpenter watches as the first lady arrives with a Secret Service agent and walks to the head table.

Ms. Carpenter: "There was much expectation about Mrs. Kennedy, hoping that she would come because she did have a 'Grace Kelly attraction' and everyone was eager to see her.

"One of the public information men for the governor…said to me, 'Has Jackie blown it again?' And I said, 'I'm quite sure she'll be here.'

"Sure enough, in a minute, with cameras and lights on, Mrs. Kennedy entered, looking perfectly beautiful in a pink dress with navy blue lapels and a pink pillbox hat.

"She went up all alone with her Secret Service agent beside her, but in a spectacular entrance, with great cheers from the crowd, and seated herself by the president. He didn't speak to her immediately, but the vice president got up and was very chivalrous.

"I watched carefully to see if there was any exchange, and there was briefly, but I had the feeling that he was irritated that she hadn't made the entrance with him."

Alann Bedford, wife of Fort Worth oilman Charles Bedford, is among the breakfast guests.

Mrs. Bedford: "She did walk in a little late, but that was exactly what impressed me so much. She walked in with the greatest dignity....She absolutely won my admiration."

9:25 a.m.

Willard Barr, Fort Worth's mayor pro tem, remembers that many of the guests were Chamber of Commerce members and businessmen.

Barr: "Probably most of them would have gone out and voted against him, but he had them charmed — sort of in the palm of his hand — by the time he finished his speech.

"He started his speech with praise for Jim Wright. Of course, Jim had a lot of supporters there.

"He then went on to talk about Jacqueline. He said, 'Everybody waits to see what Jacqueline will wear, and they never pay attention to what you and I wear, Lyndon. Nobody cares what we wear.'"

9:50 a.m.

Dr. Marion Brooks, a physician and a leader in Fort Worth's black community, attends the speech only after considerable negotiation. The Chamber of Commerce initially made no tickets available to blacks but later granted 50. Brooks watches as the Kennedys are presented cowboy hats and boots.

Brooks: "When he was handed the hat, he looked at it and smiled — but he didn't put it on....He made no apologies for that....

"And I think it would have been somewhat demeaning and insulting for him to patronize us Texans and the rest by playing like he wanted a cowboy hat."

9:55 a.m.

The Rev. Granville Walker, pastor of University Christian Church, gives the morning benediction.

Walker: "I used the traditional prayer of 'Lord bless you and be gracious unto you.' I added a few words about peace in the world…and I asked for the president's health to be guarded and that of his family.

"It was a routine thing to say. You wouldn't have to have any premonitions to do that."

THE EVENTS OF NOV. 22, 1963

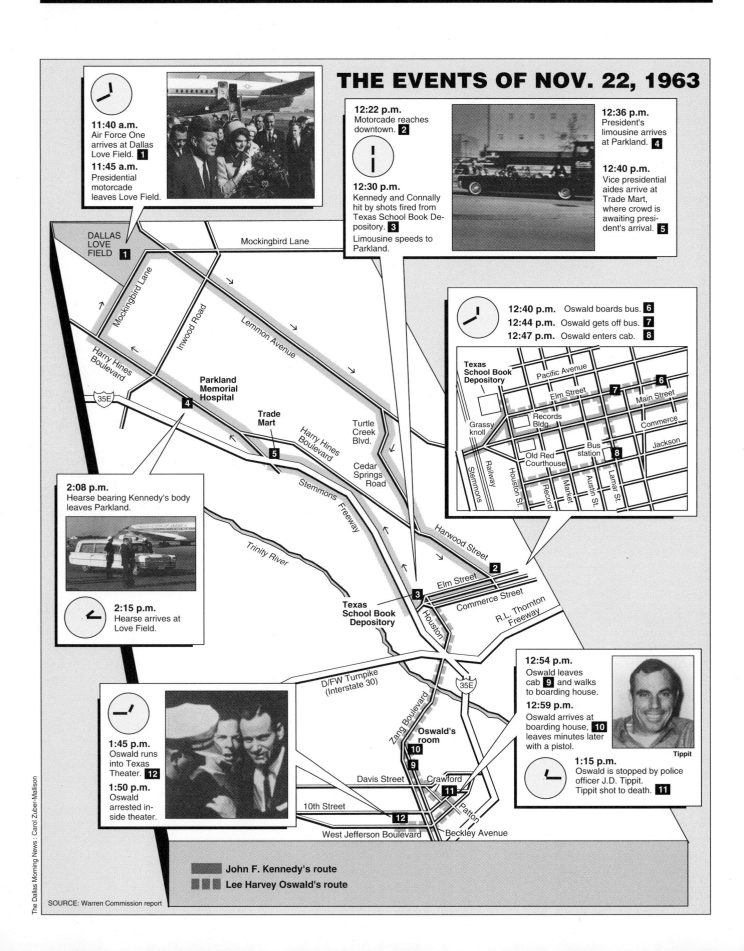

11:40 a.m. Air Force One arrives at Dallas Love Field. **1**

11:45 a.m. Presidential motorcade leaves Love Field.

12:22 p.m. Motorcade reaches downtown. **2**

12:30 p.m. Kennedy and Connally hit by shots fired from Texas School Book Depository. **3** Limousine speeds to Parkland.

12:36 p.m. President's limousine arrives at Parkland. **4**

12:40 p.m. Vice presidential aides arrive at Trade Mart, where crowd is awaiting president's arrival. **5**

12:40 p.m. Oswald boards bus. **6**
12:44 p.m. Oswald gets off bus. **7**
12:47 p.m. Oswald enters cab. **8**

2:08 p.m. Hearse bearing Kennedy's body leaves Parkland.

2:15 p.m. Hearse arrives at Love Field.

12:54 p.m. Oswald leaves cab **9** and walks to boarding house.

12:59 p.m. Oswald arrives at boarding house, **10** leaves minutes later with a pistol.

Tippit

1:15 p.m. Oswald is stopped by police officer J.D. Tippit. Tippit shot to death. **11**

1:45 p.m. Oswald runs into Texas Theater. **12**

1:50 p.m. Oswald arrested inside theater.

DALLAS LOVE FIELD **1**

Mockingbird Lane

Mockingbird Lane

Inwood Road

Lemmon Avenue

Harry Hines Boulevard

35E

Parkland Memorial Hospital **4**

Trade Mart **5**

Harry Hines Boulevard

Turtle Creek Blvd.

Cedar Springs Road

Stemmons Freeway

Trinity River

Harwood Street

Elm Street

Commerce Street

Texas School Book Depository **3**

Houston

2

R.L. Thornton Freeway

D/FW Turnpike (Interstate 30)

35E

Zang Boulevard

Oswald's room **10** **9**

Davis Street

Crawford

11

Patton

10th Street

12

West Jefferson Boulevard

Beckley Avenue

Texas School Book Depository

Pacific Avenue

Elm Street **7**

Main Street **6**

Records Bldg.

Commerce

Grassy knoll

Bus station **8**

Jackson

Railway

Stemmons

Houston St.

Old Red Courthouse

Record

Market

Lamar St.

Austin St.

John F. Kennedy's route

Lee Harvey Oswald's route

The Dallas Morning News : Carol Zuber-Mallison

SOURCE: Warren Commission report

10:14 a.m.

The Kennedys arrive at their suite to prepare for the motorcade to Carswell Air Force Base. The president phones John Nance Garner, former vice president under Franklin D. Roosevelt, in Uvalde to congratulate him on his 95th birthday. An aide shows the president a full-page ad that appeared that day in The Dallas Morning News. The ad is critical of his presidency.

10:40 a.m.

The motorcade travels to Carswell for the short flight to Dallas. Kennedy aide O'Brien ensures that Yarborough is in the car with Johnson. The two Texans have been at odds before, and headlines this morning suggest that Yarborough has been snubbing Johnson during the president's trip.

O'Brien: "I pointed out to Ralph as we stood in front of the hotel and said, 'Just look down there. All the press can see you, Ralph. And it's in the forefront of their thinking that this trip has to date been considerably marred by the emphasis on Yarborough-Johnson.'

"Ralph…didn't want that to be an ongoing situation, and he quite readily agreed to join Johnson in the motorcade."

10:45 a.m.

As Ms. Carpenter rides in the motorcade, her thoughts turn to Dallas — and to the pending presidential candidacy of Republican Sen. Barry Goldwater.

Ms. Carpenter: "Dallas had been, I think in the minds of everyone, a questionable spot. If we made a good show there, it really meant that all of the Goldwater talk was nothing because it (Dallas) was the most anti-Johnson, the most anti-Democratic and the most anti-everything in Texas."

11:10 a.m.

Departure from Carswell is delayed by a

At Dallas' Love Field, Mrs. Kennedy carries a bouquet of red roses given to her by Dearie Cabell, wife of Mayor Earle Cabell.

The Dallas Morning News

spontaneous show of support from Air Force personnel. Kennedy shakes hands with the Fort Worth delegation, and speaks with Sheriff Evans and Fort Worth Mayor Bayard Friedman, a staunch Republican.

Evans: "He said, 'Sheriff, you've got a wonderful place to live here — try to keep it that way.'"

Friedman: "I remember my wife had on some unusual triangular-shaped earrings, and he commented on their beauty. Of course, that was almost enough to have gotten her vote."

11:20 a.m.

Kennedy departs on Air Force One; Johnson flies out on Air Force Two.

About 11:40 a.m.

Waiting at Dallas Love Field are Police Chief Jesse Curry and Capt. Glen King. Dallas minister Baxton Bryant, a leader of liberal-loyalist Democrats, has assembled hundreds of supporters to welcome Kennedy.

Bryant: "I talked to Kennedy, and he was amazed at how many people were there.…Kennedy said, 'This doesn't look like an anti-Kennedy crowd.'"

Ms. Carpenter: "I remember the ugly look of one man sitting on top of a car who wanted to make no mistake that his sign was read. It was a glaring sign with a lot of lettered charges against the Kennedy administration.…I felt he had sat there a long time — just really to show hatred.

"However, the fabulous thing about the Dallas reception was it was not at all as we

The Dallas Morning News

The presidential limousine moves along Main Street in downtown Dallas.

Sanders: "The crowd started building. From Ervay Street on, the crowds were very thick and very friendly. The chatter on the bus was, 'Gee, isn't this nice? Isn't this a pretty day?'"

Jack Valenti, a Houston public relations man accompanying Johnson, is aboard the bus.

Valenti: "I recall we were all remarking about how marvelous the reception was.…There were no hostile faces, not even a hostile sign, which was amazing."

Lady Bird Johnson rides with the vice president and Sen. Yarborough.

Mrs. Johnson: "The streets were lined with people — lots and lots of people — the children all smiling, placards, confetti, people waving from windows."

About 12:15 p.m.

At the Trade Mart, many of the 2,600 guests are arriving for the 12:30 p.m. speech. Erik Jonsson, president of the Dallas Citizens Council, has gone straight to the Trade Mart from Love Field to make final preparations.

Jonsson: "Everything was in order. We even had presents purchased for the president's two children.…One was a big teddy bear for little John; the other was for Caroline, but I can't recall what it was.

"Everything was organized as well as we knew how to do it."

12:29 p.m.

The caravan is about to turn north on Houston Street. As the car passes the Dallas County Courthouse, Nellie Connally is moved by the reaction of the spectators and turns to the president.

envisioned — just thousands of people. They outdid San Antonio and outdid Houston and outdid Fort Worth."

11:45 a.m.

Charles Roberts, a Newsweek *correspondent covering the presidential party, watches as Kennedy enters the back seat of his convertible limousine. Mrs. Kennedy sits beside her husband. Secret Service agent Bill Greer is driving; agent Roy Kellerman sits beside him. Gov. Connally and his wife, Nellie, take the jump seats. The other cars in the entourage fall in behind for the motorcade that will take them through downtown Dallas en route to the Trade Mart, where Kennedy is to deliver a luncheon address.*

Roberts: "He (Kennedy) had inquired about the weather that morning and decided that they would not have the top on it (the limousine). They had a choice of three tops: a fabric top — a fabric top,

of course, would have obscured him from the public; and the plastic top, which the Secret Service had told me would deflect a bullet but would not stop it; and then a metal top."

About 11:50 a.m.

Kennedy halts the motorcade at the intersection of Lemmon Avenue and Lomo Alto Drive to greet a group of small children.

Connally: "There was one little girl…who was carrying a sign saying, 'Mr. President, will you please stop and shake hands with me?'…He just told the driver to stop…and, of course, he was immediately mobbed by a bunch of youngsters."

About noon

U.S. Attorney Barefoot Sanders shares a bus with about 20 people, mostly White House staff members. The bus is several vehicles behind the presidential limousine.

Mrs. Connally: "Mr. Kennedy, you can't say that Dallas doesn't love you."

12:30 p.m.

The limousine travels down the slope in front of the book depository at the northwest corner of Houston and Elm. Shots ring out.

Mrs. Kennedy: "I heard these terrible noises…and my husband never made a sound.…He had this sort of quizzical look on his face.…I remember thinking he just looked as if he had a slight headache.…

"I remember falling on him and saying…'Oh, my God, they have shot my husband.' And 'I love you Jack.' I remember I was shouting."

Secret Service agent Clint Hill, in the next car back in the motorcade, bolts for the president's limousine.

Hill: "I heard a noise.…I saw President Kennedy grab at himself and lurch forward.…

"Mrs. Kennedy…jumped up from the seat…when she noticed that I was trying to climb on the car. She turned toward me, and I grabbed her and put her back in the back seat, crawled up on top of the back seat and lay there."

Connally: "Strangely, I had but one thought — this is an assassination attempt.…

"When I was hit, I said, 'Oh, no, no, no.' And then I said, 'My God, they are trying to kill us all.'"

Mrs. Connally: "I pulled him (Connally) over into my arms and put my head down on his. I thought he was dead. But then he moved his hand — it was an almost imperceptible movement — and I knew he was alive."

Bill and Gayle Newman have brought their two young sons downtown to see the president. They are standing along the curb on Elm Street in front of the grassy knoll.

Mrs. Newman: "This shot fired out, and I thought it was a firecracker, and the

At 12:30 p.m. President Kennedy is struck by a bullet.

The president slumps; Connally turns in his seat.

president kind of raised up in his seat, and I thought, you know, he was kind of going along with a gag or something. And then all of a sudden the next one popped…and another one — it was just all so fast.…And my husband said, 'Quick, get down,' and I grabbed the baby, and we ran and laid down on the grass and I got on top of him."

Secret Service agent Rufus Youngblood is riding with the Johnsons.

Youngblood: "I turned instinctively in my seat, and with my left hand I grasped Lyndon Johnson's right shoulder, and with all the leverage I could exert from a sitting position, I forced him downward.

"'Get down!' I shouted. 'Get down!' The vice president reacted immediately.

A second shot strikes the president.

The mortally wounded president falls toward his wife.

Still not seeing the source of the explosion, I swung across the back seat and sat on top of him."

Mrs. Johnson: "Then in the lead car, the Secret Service men were suddenly down. I heard over the radio system, 'Let's get out of here!'

"The car accelerated terrifically fast — faster and faster."

Seconds after 12:30 p.m.

Merriman Smith of United Press Interna-tional, riding in the front seat of the press pool car, grabs the radio-phone on the dashboard. Jack Bell of The Associated Press and Robert Baskin, Washington bureau chief of The Dallas Morning News, are in the back seat.

Baskin: "People could be seen diving for the ground, some protecting their children with their bodies.…

"Smith grabbed the telephone.…Jack Bell began to demand the telephone as we raced along, but Smith would not relin-quish it.…A wrestling match for the phone ensued."

Several bystanders point to the upper levels of the seven-story book depository. Police rush into the building to conduct a search. Car salesman James T. Tague is among the spectators standing across from the book depository.

Tague: "There was a man sobbing, 'His head exploded,' and at that point we determined he was talking about the presi-dent's head and that he had been killed. I remember (Deputy Sheriff) Buddy Wal-ters kicking the grass, saying, 'Oh damn, oh damn.'

"And at that time, he looked at me and he says, 'You've got blood on your face.' And I reached up and there were a couple of drops of blood on my cheek, and I recalled that during the shooting some-thing had stung my face."

12:33 p.m.

The phone rings in the emergency room of Parkland Memorial Hospital. Doris Nelson, a registered nurse, answers the call.

Ms. Nelson: "The operator told me the president had been shot. I thought she was joking and asked her what else was new. But then, from the tone of her voice, I knew she wasn't kidding. She said the president's motorcade was on its way to Parkland."

12:34 p.m.

UPI transmits Merriman Smith's 12-word bulletin around the world: "THREE SHOTS WERE FIRED AT PRESIDENT KENNEDY'S MOTORCADE TODAY IN DOWNTOWN DALLAS."

The bulletin touches off bells on a U.S. State Department Boeing 707 over the Pacific. Heading for a Tokyo trade conference are Secretary of State Dean Rusk, Treasury Sec-retary Douglas Dillon, Secretary of Com-merce Luther H. Hodges, Secretary of Agri-culture Orville Freeman, Secretary of Labor

Willard Wirtz and Secretary of the Interior Stewart Udall.

Also on the aircraft are deputy White House counsel Myer Feldman and White House press secretary Pierre Salinger, who speaks by radio to the Situation Room in the White House.

Salinger: "Please listen hard — this plane on which Secretary of State Rusk and other Cabinet members are headed for Japan is turning around and returning to Honolulu. Will arrive there in approximately two hours....Any other information, please get...as quickly as possible."

Situation Room: "The AP is coming out now to the effect that they believe the president was hit in the head. That just came in."

Salinger: "Hit in the head?"

Situation Room: "Roger. Will pass on any additional information we get as soon as we hear it."

Feldman: "Dean Rusk...and the other Cabinet members and I gathered in the front of the plane and decided the only thing to do was to turn back. At that point, we didn't know that he had been killed — just that he had been shot. So we turned around to come back.

"I looked at Orville Freeman, I remember, and Orville had been shot at Guadalcanal. The bullet had gone from just below his jaw up through his skull, and he had survived....I said, 'Well, if you could have survived that, I think the president could survive a shot.'

"It was after we had turned the plane around to come back that we found he had been killed, and then our concern was as to where the vice president was and where the speaker was because Dean Rusk was fourth in line.

"We thought this might be a Russian plot and if it was a Russian plot, then we were all in danger, too."

12:36 p.m.

The presidential limousine arrives at Parkland. The car carrying the Johnsons and Yarborough follows.

Mrs. Kennedy rises in the rear seat of the limousine.

Secret Service Agent Clint Hill climbs onto the car.

Mrs. Johnson: "We pulled up to a building. I looked up and saw it said 'Hospital.' Only then did I believe that this might be what it was.

"Secret Service men began to pull, lead, guide and hustle us out. I cast one last look over my shoulder and saw, in the president's car, a bundle of pink, just like a drift of blossoms, lying on the back seat. I think it was Mrs. Kennedy lying over the president's body."

Yarborough: "The minute the car stopped, the Secret Service rushed at Johnson and formed a cordon around him....I heard one of them say 'Mr. President' to Johnson, and I knew then Kennedy was dead....

"I got up and walked up to the Kennedy car, and Mrs. Kennedy was sit-

The Dallas Morning News

After the shots, photographers on the grassy knoll dash after the speeding motorcade. Bill and Gayle Newman shield their children.

ting there with President Kennedy's head in her lap. I didn't say anything. There was too much agony.

"And I heard her say twice: 'They murdered my husband; they murdered my husband.'"

12:38 p.m.

Dr. Charles R. Baxter, professor of surgery at the University of Texas Southwestern Medical School and director of Parkland's emergency room, stands by in Trauma Room One with Dr. William Kemp Clark, a neurosurgeon.

Baxter: "The president's care was aimed at stabilizing breathing and stopping bleeding first so that other wounds could be treated. Within only a few minutes, it

was obvious that the situation for the president was hopeless.

"He started to have a cardiac arrest. But we did not resuscitate him because Dr. Clark had examined his head wound and said it was hopeless.

"As soon as we knew we had nothing medical to do, we all backed off from the man with a reverence that one has for one's president. And we did not continue to be doctors from that point on. We became citizens again, and there were probably more tears shed in that room than in the surrounding hundred miles."

Clark: "There was a delay in the notification of death to honor Mrs. Kennedy's wish that a priest be allowed to give last rites before the president was pronounced dead."

12:40 p.m.

The Johnsons sit in a small waiting room at Parkland.

Mrs. Johnson: "There was talk about where we would go — back to Washington, to the plane, to our house. People spoke of how widespread this may be. Through it all, Lyndon was remarkably calm and quiet....

"He said, 'You better try to see if you can see Jackie and Nellie.'

"(Secret Service agents) began to lead me up one corridor, back stairs and down another. Suddenly I found myself face to face with Jackie in a small hall. I think it was right outside the operating room.

"You always think of her or someone like her as being insulated, protected. She

The presidential limousine races toward Parkland Memorial Hospital, passing the Trade Mart on Stemmons Freeway, where a crowd waits to hear the president's planned speech.

Two employees peer from the Texas School Book Depository, below the window where the shots were fired.

Dallas police officers, with their guns ready, look up at the School Book Depository.

Boxes frame the sixth-floor hiding place of the sniper who fired at the motorcade.

was quite alone. I don't think I ever saw anyone so much alone in my life. I went up to her, put my arms around her and said something...like 'God help us all.'"

Johnson's secretary, Marie Fehmer, and other vice presidential aides arrive at the Trade Mart. Their bus had become separated from the motorcade after the shots were fired.

Ms. Fehmer: "When we got there, we were just lost souls who happened to be deposited at the Trade Mart, and nobody would tell us anything....I knew that if there was a problem, they would go to the hospital. I knew the nearest hospital was Parkland, so I literally commandeered a police car, told the officer who we were and said, 'Please take us to Parkland.'...

"We were saying our rosaries on the way to the hospital."

Vice presidential political adviser Cliff Carter is with Johnson when Kennedy aide Kenneth O'Donnell enters the room.

Carter: "Ken O'Donnell had come in and was giving the VP the estimate of the situation, and the VP asked what was the president's condition. Ken said, 'He's gone.'"

Shortly after 12:40 p.m.

Lee Harvey Oswald's wife, Marina, hears of the shooting from Ruth Paine, who shares her Irving home with Marina and her two daughters. Oswald, who lives in an Oak Cliff rooming house, visits on weekends.

The Dallas Morning News

Dearie Cabell, the wife of Dallas Mayor Earle Cabell, waits in a motorcade car outside Parkland Hospital.

to Union Station, so she got off the bus; Oswald got off the bus with her.

"He didn't say anything; he just got off the bus."

Oswald walks to the Greyhound bus station, where he takes a cab to Beckley and Neely, a five-minute walk from his Oak Cliff rooming house.

12:45 p.m.

Dr. Baxter moves to the operating room where Connally is being treated.

Baxter: "John Connally had a lethal wound, and it went totally unnoticed — except by the people who were treating Mr. Connally — because of the emphasis on the president. But he (Connally) had a sucking chest wound; the side of his chest was blown out. And he was blue and agonal (near death) when he arrived at the emergency room."

Dr. Kenneth Pepper, a Parkland chaplain, spends much of the rest of the day with Nellie Connally.

Pepper: "Mrs. Connally was afraid he (Connally) would not be treated because all the movement was around Kennedy."

About 12:50 p.m.

Steve Landregan, an assistant administrator at Parkland, is near the major surgery area.

Landregan: "Mrs. Nelson (the registered nurse) motioned me over and whispered, 'He's dead.'...A Secret Service man with no coat on and a bloody shirt came over to me and said, 'We've got to get a coffin.' I gave the Secret Service man my coat to cover his bloody shirt; he said he had to put his over the president....

"I went back to the major surgery area, where I was standing next to Mayor (Earle) Cabell and overheard him saying to no one in particular, 'It didn't happen; it didn't happen.'"

Marina Oswald: "Ruth came in and told me they were saying that the shots came from the building where Lee works, and this frozen feeling came over me. I knew it might be him. I ran outside and started hanging up diapers so she (Mrs. Paine) wouldn't see my face turn red. I was flushed."

Dallas Transit System bus driver Cecil J. McWatters is heading west on Elm Street, about seven blocks from the book depository, his bus half-filled.

McWatters: "Three men, including Oswald, got on the bus. They were more or less running to catch the bus. But that wasn't unusual; people were always in a hurry to catch the bus.

"Oswald was sitting three or four seats back from the front. He had a hole in his shirt, and his elbow was sticking out of it. We pulled out from the curb, and traffic began to get backed up. We went another block down Elm, and finally we got bogged in the traffic.

"While we were sitting there, a man ahead of us got out of his car and came up to the bus and said he had heard on the radio that the president had been shot. I turned around and told the people on the bus....One woman was in a hurry to get

U.S. Rep. Henry B. Gonzalez, a San Antonio Democrat who had ridden in the motorcade, arrives at Parkland.

Gonzalez: "I…went over to the limousine and looked down in horror at the blood-soaked seat and floorboard and the trampled roses, and I said, 'My God, Mrs. Kennedy was hit.' I still didn't want to believe the president was shot."

Gonzalez sees Mrs. Kennedy in a hospital waiting room, finds a cigarette for her and offers her a glass of water.

Gonzalez: "She had a very, well, not aristocratic, but a classic way of saying 'Thank you.' She was just like she was in a trance.…

"All of a sudden an attendant in white opens the door where I was standing and there I see this bed, this body with a linen sheet not fully covering the palms or the bottoms of his feet.

"It suddenly dawned on me that that was the president, and then tears came to my eyes, and I couldn't control myself.…

"They called Mrs. Kennedy, and she came in there and she kissed the body and she took her ring off and put it on (the president's finger).…Then they rolled out the coffin."

Still at the Trade Mart, Erik Jonsson is concerned about the delay in Kennedy's arrival.

Jonsson: "It began to be apparent that something was amiss, but nobody thought much about it at first. Pretty soon, we got word from somebody that there had been shots. Perhaps an assassination attempt.

"I asked them to go ahead with the luncheon.…We still had no solid information."

Word reaches the Trade Mart that the president has been killed. Rumors begin to circulate, including one that Vice President Johnson has been shot. Among those at the luncheon are Dallas lawyer Grier Raggio and Dallas school Superintendent W.T. White.

The Dallas Morning News

A bouquet of yellow roses — given earlier to Nellie Connally — lies on the floor of the presidential limousine outside Parkland.

Raggio: "I was very, very upset, as were most of the others.…People were crying there and saying to other people they thought it was an assassination, a planned assassination by the so-called rightists, so-called Republicans.

"And they were saying, that's gone too far."

White: "Everybody got quiet and just walked out. One of the women was hysterical. She said, 'I guess now the so-and-sos will be glad because the president is dead.' I didn't know who she was talking about. I just walked on."

12:57 p.m.

As parish priest of Parkland, the Rev. Oscar Huber of Holy Trinity Catholic Church rushes to the hospital with his assistant, the Rev. James N. Thompson.

Huber: "He was covered with a sheet, which I removed from over his forehead before administering conditionally the last rites of the Catholic Church. These rites are administered conditionally when a priest has no way of knowing the person's

The Dallas Morning News

Assistant press secretary Malcolm Kilduff, Kennedy's chief spokesman on the Texas trip, announces to reporters gathered at Parkland hospital that the president has been pronounced dead.

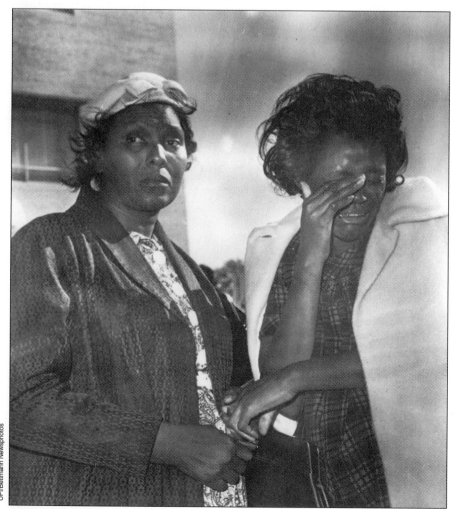

UPI/Bettmann Newsphotos

An unidentified woman outside Parkland Hospital weeps at the news of Kennedy's death.

mind or whether the soul has yet left the body....'Eternal rest grant unto him, O Lord, and let perpetual light shine upon him. May he rest in peace. Amen.'

"Mrs. Kennedy bent over and seemed to kiss the president....During this most trying ordeal, the perfect composure maintained by Mrs. Kennedy was beyond comprehension. I will never forget the blank stare in her eyes and the signs of agony on her face....In a low voice, she thanked me graciously and asked me to pray for the president."

Thompson: "I noticed the gloved hand of the president's wife was saturated with blood....Just for a moment I wished I could just pick her up, carry her away, saying, 'This isn't true — it's just a bad dream.'...I went to the president's wife, took her hand, and in the best way I could, offered my condolences....

"Having just left Parkland, suddenly I was aware that my right hand was sticking to the steering wheel. Then I realized, just as sudden as the president's death, that I had the blood of a president on my hand. My God."

12:59 p.m.

Oswald arrives at his rooming house in Oak Cliff. He grabs his pistol and leaves several minutes later.

1 p.m.

President John Fitzgerald Kennedy is pronounced dead by Dr. Clark. Assistant press secretary Malcolm Kilduff, the president's chief spokesman on the Texas trip, tells Kennedy aide O'Donnell that the president's death must be announced.

Kilduff: "He said, 'Don't ask me, ask Johnson.' Not Lyndon, not the president — Johnson. So I went and I found Lyndon Johnson...across the hall from the emergency room....I walked up to him and I didn't know what to call him. I didn't know him that well, so I wasn't about to call him Lyndon. And he wasn't vice president, he was de facto president.

So I just walked up to him and I said, 'Mr. President.' And Lady Bird screamed, kind of an audible yelp. Nobody had bothered to tell them."

1:05 p.m.

Aboard the Cabinet plane, which had aborted its trip to Japan and turned back toward Hawaii, Salinger has been in continuous contact with the White House Situation Room since learning of the shooting.

Salinger: "After about 30 minutes, a voice came on: 'Wayside, stand by.' Wayside was my code name. About every 30 seconds for the next three or four minutes the voice would come back, 'Wayside, stand by.' Then finally, a voice, 'Wayside, Lancer is dead.' Lancer was the president's code name."

1:15 p.m.

Dallas police officer J.D. Tippit is shot in Oak Cliff. Ted Callaway, a used-car salesman at a lot near 10th Street and Patton Avenue, hears the shots.

Callaway: "I could tell they were coming from right behind us....I ran to the corner. Oswald was running toward me on the sidewalk. He had run through a 6-foot hedge at the corner where the policeman was shot.

"He had a pistol in his right hand....He pointed the gun at me; he slowed down as he ran toward me. I asked, 'Hey man, what's going on?' He didn't say a word; he just shrugged his shoulders.

"I ran to the corner to find out what was going on. The officer was on the ground. He was lying on his back. He had drawn his pistol or it had fallen out of his holster, because it was lying by his right arm. He had been shot in the face and chest, and I could tell he was a dead man."

L.J. Lewis, also a used-car salesman, sees a man running along Patton Avenue shortly after hearing gunfire.

Lewis: "I saw a man coming down the street reloading his revolver. He had a coat down over his arm. I called the police....He ran into an alley. Some of the men followed him. Some of them found his coat there."

1:16 p.m.

Dallas police officer M.N. "Nick" McDonald, one of about 25 officers assigned to control the crowd outside the book depository, hears on his radio that an officer driving Unit 10 has been shot in Oak Cliff.

McDonald: "I knew immediately that was J.D. Tippit's squad car. I knew him. We dressed side by side in the police locker room in the southwest substation. He was a neighbor of mine, lived a block from me over in Oak Cliff.

"I reported to the supervisor and asked for permission to leave the scene and go to Oak Cliff to search for a suspect who shot J.D. Tippit. They had plenty of officers to take care of what they were doing, anyway."

Assistant District Attorney Bill Alexander, also at the book depository, hears the same radio report.

Dallas police officer J.D. Tippit, who confronted Oswald in Oak Cliff.

Alexander: "Bud Owens (a Dallas police officer) had his car parked there....There was a mention that he was solo, and I said I'd go with him."

1:22 p.m.

Book depository officials poll their employees and discover that Oswald is missing. Police find a rifle at the depository.

The corner of Tenth Street and Patton Avenue, where Tippit was shot.

Associated Press

The Texas Theater, where Lee Harvey Oswald was found and arrested, is shown in a photo taken that evening.

1:30 p.m.

Liz Carpenter rides to Love Field in another police car.

Ms. Carpenter: "I started thinking that one thing I could do was to start writing what the vice president would have to say when he stepped off a plane.

"With a pencil, I started writing out a statement and, as it turns out, most of it was what the vice president used with a few little changes."

1:31 p.m.

Kilduff announces to the press that Kennedy is dead.

1:33 p.m.

Johnson boards Air Force One and meets with aides. The pilot is Air Force Col. James B. Swindal; also aboard are Johnson's secretary, Ms. Fehmer, and Valenti, the Houston public relations man.

Mrs. Johnson: "We entered airplane Number One for the first time. There was a TV set on, and the commentator was saying, 'Lyndon B. Johnson, now president of the United States.'"

Valenti: "We were sitting there some time when suddenly he (Johnson) appeared in this passageway, looming over us. We all stood up automatically. Even in that instant there was a new demeanor in all of us, and certainly in Johnson.

"I often thought that he looked graver. Whatever emotions or passions he had in him, he had put them under strict discipline. He was very quiet and seemingly very much in command of himself."

Swindal: "Mr. Johnson stated that he would not leave for Washington without Mrs. Kennedy and the body of the president."

Ms. Fehmer: "(Johnson) was, first of all, a Southern gentleman, regardless of the salty language and the masculine behavior. He was sincerely concerned about Mrs.

Alexander: "En route over there (to Oak Cliff), the police radio was broadcasting that Oswald was missing, and we were also getting a description of the man who shot Tippit."

1:26 p.m.

An entourage of Secret Service agents, the Johnsons, and U.S. Reps. Homer Thornberry and Jack Brooks leave Parkland for Love Field to board Air Force One. Police Chief Curry drives the unmarked police car in which Johnson rides.

Curry: "I don't know whether he was on the floor or whether he was just lying down in the seat, but he was low, as low as he could get in the car, on instructions of his bodyguards.

"We didn't know whether this was an organized conspiracy, (whether) there'd be others who they would attempt to assassinate, or just what the situation was."

Mrs. Johnson: "We drove along as fast as we could.

"I looked up at a building and there already was a flag at half-mast. I think that is when the enormity of what had happened first struck me."

Dallas police officer M.N. "Nick" McDonald arrested Oswald after a struggle in the Texas Theater.

Associated Press

Officers remove Oswald from the theater.

Warren Commission

Kennedy and the president's body and wanted to make sure they were returned safely to Washington.

"Others, particularly the Secret Service men, were talking about the need for protection and security and, thus, the need to return to Washington immediately. But he kept saying, 'That is what I have to do. I owe it to that woman and her husband.'"

About 1:45 p.m.

Warren Burroughs, working behind the concession stand at the Texas Theater in Oak Cliff, sees Oswald rush in without buying a ticket. Police arrive minutes later, and employees show officer McDonald where Oswald is sitting.

Burroughs: "He (Oswald) darted up the stairs to the balcony....The police ran up the balcony, but he had already come down the back stairs. There were about 18 people in the auditorium. He was sitting by a pregnant lady who got up to go to the restroom. The police came from both sides."

McDonald: "I was going to search every person as I came to them before I got to him, so I wouldn't make a mistake or overlook anybody or anything else that might be connected.

"I was looking at Oswald over my right shoulder, glancing at him, seeing what he was doing, making sure he was still in one place. I gave these guys a pat search. I had them sit back down and I walked... toward Oswald.

"I was trying to show an act of diversion so as Oswald may think I wasn't even considering him.

"And as soon as I got to him — I was just inches from him — I said, 'Get on your feet.' He stood up, and he said, 'Well, it's all over now.'

"He was bringing his hands up at this point....Suddenly (he) made a fist and hit me between the eyes with his left fist and in the same motion drew a pistol from his waist....

"I happened to grab the pistol over the cylinder....As we fell into the seats, I could feel the hammer come back on his pistol. And then it returned. The firing pin on the hammer struck me on the hand between the forefinger and thumb.

"This, of course, retarded the action of the hammer, and the bullet didn't receive the full force....I managed to get my right hand on the butt of the pistol, and I jerked it away....

"I stuck the gun into his stomach for just an instant....I thought about shooting him. The thought came through my

mind, 'This guy's trying to kill me. I'll try to kill him.'

"Then I said to myself, 'Well, we don't need to shoot him because I've got him now. He's under control.'"

1:50 p.m.

Detective Bob Carroll helps McDonald escort Oswald from the theater.

Carroll: "There was a crowd outside the picture show when we brought him out — a dozen or so folks there. They were yelling, 'Kill that son of a bitch! Let us have him. We'll kill him.'"

At Parkland, Medical Examiner Earl Rose, Justices of the Peace David L. Johnston and Theron Ward, and Parkland official Landregan argue with Secret Service agents about removing Kennedy's body. Rose points out that Texas law says an autopsy must be performed in a violent death. Kennedy's aides, including O'Brien, enter the discussion.

Landregan: "I noticed Dr. Earl Rose attempting to make out the necessary legal papers for removal of the body. He seemed quite agitated and upset and was asking for Judge Ward. During the next

The Dallas Morning News

At Parkland hospital, Jacqueline Kennedy enters the hearse bearing the body of her slain husband.

few minutes…(there) seemed to be some question as to whether or not an autopsy would be ordered on the president."

Johnston: "The turmoil was there. It wasn't as bad as some people would try to make you believe. Some federal agents got a little testy."

O'Brien: "The local coroner, whoever he may have been, and somebody who described himself, as I recall, as a judge, were saying that the coffin couldn't be moved. And Jackie said, 'I'm not leaving without Jack.'"

2 p.m.

Aboard Air Force One at Love Field, Johnson phones Attorney General Robert Kennedy in Washington.

Johnson: "I talked to the attorney general (and) asked him what we should

do…where I should take the oath…here or there.…(He) said he would like to look into it and would notify me whether we should take it here or not.

"McGeorge Bundy (special assistant to Kennedy) and Walter (Jenkins, a Johnson aide) called me (and) thought we should come to Washington as soon as (we) could. (I) told them I was waiting for the body and Mrs. Kennedy. The attorney general interrupted the conversation to say that I ought to have a judicial officer administer the oath here."

Ms. Fehmer: "I called Judge Sarah Hughes' office. They said she was not there. The president said that he'd talk to anyone in her office. He got on the phone and told the person at the other end that he needed someone to administer the oath and to find her and get her to Love Field.…

"Dave Powers (a Kennedy aide) and Ken O'Donnell came into the stateroom. The president quickly swallowed a bowl of vegetable soup and ate crackers.

"The president looked at Dave Powers and said, 'It's been a week since I got up.'"

John A. Spinuzzi, a law clerk for U.S. District Judge Sarah T. Hughes, answers the call from Ms. Fehmer.

Spinuzzi: "I think the phone rested on the cradle 20 seconds, and it rang again. It was Vice President Johnson.…He said, 'I want Sarah Hughes to meet me at the airport. President Kennedy is dead, and I want her to swear me in. I don't care what you have to do — find her.'

"About 20 to 25 minutes later, she just by chance called in. She immediately asked us to locate the oath of office."

The hearse arrives at Love Field, and the president's body is placed aboard Air Force One.

U.S. Attorney Sanders: "She didn't have an oath. She said, 'If you don't have one, I'll get one figured out,' and she would have. I didn't hear any more except that I couldn't find the cotton-picking oath of office."

Spinuzzi: "That was kind of infuriating. We had all the so-called legal talent there, and we couldn't find it."

"It's in the Constitution."

Col. Swindal: "It took…quite a little bit (for Judge Hughes to get to the plane) with everyone on the airplane and the curtains drawn so no one could see in from outside. We didn't want to take any chances on snipers being around."

2:08 p.m.

Dallas patrol officer James Jennings helps place the president's coffin into a hearse outside Parkland. Roberts, the Newsweek *correspondent, looks on.*

Roberts: "The coffin was on one of these little rubber-tired dollies, and Mrs. Kennedy was walking on the right side of it. She was walking with her left hand on the coffin and a completely glazed look on her face, obviously in shock.…

"I had a feeling that if somebody had literally fired a pistol in front of her face that she would just have blinked.…

"They put the bronze coffin in the back door of the hearse. The curtains of it were drawn, and Mrs. Kennedy insisted on riding in the back of the hearse."

Jennings: "I put it in the back of the hearse. I took her (Mrs. Kennedy) up to the front seat of the hearse and opened the door. She started to get in and then said, 'No, I don't want to ride here. I want to ride back there (with the coffin).'"

2:12 p.m.

Judge Hughes boards Air Force One.

Judge Hughes: "I walked on into the second compartment, and there were a lot of people there.…None of us said anything. Mr. and Mrs. Johnson have been my friends for many years, but on such an occasion there did not seem to be anything to say. I embraced both of them, for that was the best way to give expression to my feelings of grief."

2:15 p.m.

The hearse arrives at Love Field. Mrs. Kennedy and members of the White House staff board Air Force One.

Col. Swindal: "The coffin bearing the body of the 35th president of the United States was brought aboard and placed in the aft compartment. A partition and four seats had been hurriedly removed."

Shortly after 2:15 p.m.

The Johnsons go to Mrs. Kennedy's cabin.

Mrs. Johnson: "She said, 'Oh, what if I had not been there. I'm so glad I was there.'

"I looked at her. Mrs. Kennedy's dress was stained with blood. Her right glove was caked — that immaculate woman — it was caked with blood, her husband's blood.

"And then, with something — if, with a person that gentle, that dignified, you can say had an element of fierceness — she said, 'I want them to see what they have done to Jack.'"

Frazier, who had taken Oswald to work that morning, listens to his radio as he drives to an Irving hospital to visit his stepfather.

Frazier: "Listening to the news, they knew more then, nearly two hours later, and they'd come to the conclusion that the only person missing in the building there was Lee.…They said they thought the person they were looking for was a young man in his 20s who had recently come from the Soviet Union.

"Riding along, I said, 'Oh God, that can't be true.' But the description they gave of him — I knew that fit Lee."

Oswald is taken to police headquarters, where detective Gus Rose is assigned to interview him about Tippit's death.

Rose: "I took his handcuffs off and sat down and started talking to him. He was belligerent and arrogant, cussed a lot, cussed me, refused to tell me who he was or his name. I searched him and found two pieces of identification — one had the name 'A. Hidell' or 'Alex Hidell,' and the other had the name Lee Oswald.

"I asked him who he was, and he said, 'You're the detective, you figure it out.' I continued to talk to him and he continued to tell me lies."

Gamma

With Mrs. Johnson and Mrs. Kennedy at his side, Johnson takes the oath of office, administered by U.S. District Judge Sarah T. Hughes on Air Force One.

Detective Capt. Will Fritz, head of the homicide and robbery bureau, interrupts Rose's questioning.

Rose: "He (Fritz) said…(they) had accounted for all the employees but one…and I want you to find him. I said, 'Well, I've got the man in here who killed officer Tippit.'

"He said, 'We'll have somebody work that out, but I want you to go find this missing man from the depository.' I said, 'Who is he?'

"He kind of fished around in his pocket and came out with a piece of paper and said, 'His name's Lee Oswald.'

"I said, 'Well, that's who we've got in the room.'"

Shortly after 2:30 p.m.

Johnson is about to take the oath.

O'Brien: "Johnson asked me if I thought Mrs. Kennedy would want to be present for this oath, and I went into the bedroom and the bathroom door was closed. So I went out and asked Evelyn Lincoln if she would check with Mrs. Kennedy, and I picked up, without really even knowing what I was doing, a Bible (actually a Catholic missal) on the stand alongside the bed in the bedroom. I brought it out and handed it to Judge Hughes."

Ms. Carpenter: "The new president came to the back and said, 'We're going to

have the swearing-in, and I'd like anyone who wants to, come in and see it.' He especially wanted all of the Kennedy people to feel welcome if they wanted to come, and all of them were crowded in different aisles or somewhere.…

"We waited five minutes until Mrs. Kennedy came out. She seemed composed, ashen and quivering."

2:38 p.m.

The jet's idling engines nearly drown out Judge Hughes' voice as she administers the oath. Johnson's hand rests on the missal.

Mrs. Johnson: "On the plane, all the shades were lowered.…In the very narrow confines of the plane, with Jackie on his left and with her hair falling in her face, but very composed, and then Lyndon, and I was on his right…Lyndon took the oath of office."

Valenti: "In my anxiety to see this — what I knew as an historic moment — I clambered over one of the chairs…and watched the proceedings very clearly. I was very close to them.

"Her (Judge Hughes') voice cracked, and her hands were shaking. She was obviously rather in a state of…near hysteria herself. But she managed to get through it, and the president shook her hand.…

"The president kissed his wife and kissed Mrs. Kennedy on the cheek. Mrs. Kennedy's face was a mask of really passive grief, I suppose is the way you'd say it. She disappeared through the narrow passageway to the rear of the plane."

Judge Hughes: "Here was a man with the ability and determination for the task ahead.…I felt he could carry on. I told him so, and that we were behind him and he would have our sympathy and our help."

Mrs. Johnson: "I heard a Secret Service man say in the most desolate voice — and I hurt for him — 'We never lost a president in the Service.'"

2:47 p.m.

Valenti watches as Judge Hughes and others leave the plane.

Valenti: "The president turned to someone and said, 'Let's get this plane airborne.' Almost within a minute the plane began to taxi onto the runway. We were airborne."

About 3 p.m.

Johnson asks his aides to call Rose Kennedy, the slain president's mother. The call is recorded:

Rose Kennedy: "Yes, Mr. President."
President Johnson: "Mrs. Kennedy, I wish to God that there was something

Attorney General Robert F. Kennedy consoles his children on the lawn of their home in McLean, Va., after being notified of his brother's death.

that I could say to you, and I want to tell you that we're grieving with you."

Mrs. Kennedy: "Thank you very much. That's very nice. I know you loved Jack and he loved you."

Ms. Carpenter: "Almost as though he couldn't bear to be with the woman in the world who would be the most sorrowful, he said, 'Here's Lady Bird,' and handed her the phone. She said very softly, 'Mrs. Kennedy, we feel like our hearts have been cut out, but we must remember…how fortunate our country was to have your son as long as it did.'"

After 3 p.m.

During the flight back to Washington, Kennedy aides O'Brien, O'Donnell and Powers sit with Mrs. Kennedy beside the coffin in the rear of the plane.

O'Brien: "She (Mrs. Kennedy) formed in her mind a firm or strong view.…It was summed up in one comment she made on the long and sad journey back to Washington. To the three of us, she directed the comment: 'You were with him at the beginning, and you were with him at the end.'"

Powers: "I have never known so much composure in a person. She made all of us feel good. I almost broke up when she said, 'Dave, you've been with him all these years, what will you do now?'"

About 3:30 p.m.

At Dallas police headquarters, Oswald is still being questioned. District Attorney Henry Wade believes that U.S. Attorney Sanders will prosecute Oswald in the president's death, but Sanders phones.

Wade: "He said, 'You know, this is going to be your baby.' I said, 'Why? Isn't it a federal offense to kill the president?' and he said: 'The most we could charge him with is assault on the president, and the maximum penalty is five years.'

"My biggest thought was that I wanted plenty of evidence. Whoever they got, I wanted enough evidence to try them on.…You don't want any mistakes."

Air Force One has reached full speed. Rep. Brooks, a longtime Johnson friend, and O'Brien talk with the new president.

Brooks: "He was concerned, as you might suspect, with the hundreds of problems affecting running the government."

O'Brien: "(I was told) the president would like to chat with me. And the president brought up the subject that the whole world was on the edge, that we had

U.S. Attorney Barefoot Sanders discusses with Henry Wade who should prosecute Oswald.

Marina Oswald was questioned by police and told them that her husband owned a rifle.

a tremendous responsibility in terms of the nation and how we acted through this period of crisis, and that it was essential that I stay with him through this whole matter.

"I remember my reaction was, 'My God, we can't be talking about this sort of thing at this point.' And so I went back to where Mrs. Kennedy was, and we talked in low-key conversation through the trip."

Ms. Fehmer: "They (Kennedy aides) were bereft. They were suffering.

"I can remember going to one or two of them and saying, 'Can I get you some soup or broth?' It offended them, and it should have, because a few hours earlier this was their airplane — yet here I was, unknown to them and with a different accent. Oh, there was just an anger and hurt that had to be taken out somewhere, and we (Johnson aides) were there."

Mrs. Johnson: "The ride to Washington was silent, strained — each with his own thoughts. One of mine was something I had said about Lyndon a long time ago — that he's a good man in a tight spot."

About 3:45 p.m.

Assistant District Attorney Alexander receives a call from police asking for a warrant to search Oswald's room at the Oak Cliff boarding house.

Alexander: "Things at the district attorney's office were beginning to heat up. I got hold of Justice of the Peace David Johnston. I had the search warrant filled out; I met Johnston on the street by the exit from the Sheriff's Department.

"A pair of homicide officers picked us up. We did a deluxe searching job of Oswald's apartment. Actually, it was a screwed-up room. We found the holster to his gun, a couple of cameras, a bunch of Communist literature and some letters he had written.

"I had Oswald's little black book with names and addresses in it, and we were real anxious to run these people down."

4 p.m.

Capt. Fritz dispatches detectives Rose, Richard Stovall and John Adamcik to the Irving home of Ruth Paine, where Marina Oswald is staying.

Rose: "When we got to Ruth Paine's house, she had her TV on, watching the assassination. 'Course, there wasn't anything else....She was cooperative, completely, but not particularly hospitable; she didn't offer us coffee or anything....

"I told her what I was there for. She told me that she (Marina) didn't speak English.

"I said, 'What does she speak?'

"She said, 'She speaks Russian; she's a Russian citizen.'

"I was rather shocked at that. I didn't know if Captain Fritz was aware of that. I called him. Ruth Paine volunteered to interpret for me.

"I asked Marina if her husband had a rifle, and she knew where it was....So she took me through the kitchen and opened the door out into the garage....She pointed to a blanket on the floor. It was rolled up; I could see the imprint of a rifle in it.

"She said through the interpreter, 'That's the gun there.' I stepped out into the garage and picked up the blanket, and it was empty. She did seem surprised — both women seemed shocked that it was not there.

"We wanted to take her (Mrs. Paine) and Marina both to City Hall to take statements. We took them outside the house....She (Marina) created kind of a scene out there in her yard and, of course, by then all the neighbors had gathered. The thing that really sparked her protest was that we had picked up some film, movie film, that was in there. We didn't know if it was hers or his.

"As we were putting them in the car, a lady came up and identified herself as a friend. She said that her brother — believe his name was Wesley Frazier — had taken Oswald to work that morning and that he'd noticed something unusual that he'd taken to work with him....He (had seen) Oswald walk up carrying some large object wrapped in brown paper.

"He told Wesley it was curtain rods."

After 4 p.m.

The refueled Cabinet plane is flying toward Washington.

Salinger: "The flight was going to take 11 hours. You have to understand, with our mind-set — a man like that being killed — what do you do? It may shock you when I tell you I started a poker game. None of the members of the Cabinet played, of course. It was wild. Nobody was thinking. We were throwing money at each other. Anything to get out of your mind what was going on."

About 4:30 p.m.

Jonsson and other civic leaders, still at the Trade Mart, discuss the impact of the assassination on Dallas.

Jonsson: "The basic decision was that we would not hire a public relations man to cure something that we had hoped could not happen.…That was a natural thing to think about. None of us wanted to do that. I was particularly vehement about that.

"The only way out of it was to perform as people should and let them see for themselves that we were not to be pictured as a city of hate."

Shortly before 5 p.m.

Air Force One approaches Andrews Air Force Base near Washington; a U.S. Navy ambulance waits on the taxi apron.

Ms. Carpenter: "The plane got ready to land, and we were told by the president that when we landed, the coffin would be taken off first with Mrs. Kennedy and the staff members.…

"Then, he and Mrs. Johnson would get off, and then he said, 'I want my staff behind me and then the Texas members of Congress.'"

In Dallas, District Attorney Wade — Connally's roommate at the University of Texas and in the Navy — arrives at Parkland to check on the governor.

Wade: "Connally was being operated on, and I talked a little bit with Nellie.…I also talked to (former Assistant District Attorney) Jim Allen, who was down at the police station, and after they went over the evidence they had, I told them to go

Jacqueline Kennedy, with Robert Kennedy, sees the coffin placed in a U.S. Navy ambulance at Andrews Air Force Base.

ahead and accept the charge on him (Oswald) for the murder of Kennedy and also of Tippit."

5 p.m.

At Andrews, Air Force One awaits a lift to remove the coffin.

Ms. Carpenter: "As we stood there…I suddenly was aware that pushing through us was Bobby Kennedy.

"His face looked streaked with tears and absolutely stricken, and he just said as he pushed past me…'Where's Jackie? I want to be with Jackie.'"

Valenti: "(Robert Kennedy) really came racing through, neither looking to the right nor to the left, to get to the back of the plane.…

"He passed President Johnson without saying anything, going to the rear of the plane."

O'Brien talks with Robert Kennedy as they await removal of the coffin.

O'Brien: "There was a military contingent that was going to take the coffin down on a forklift off the back of the plane, and we asked them to step aside, and we proceeded…to move the coffin down and into a hearse."

Associated Press

President Lyndon Johnson, with his wife, Lady Bird, at his side, makes his first address to the nation after arriving at Andrews Air Force Base.

Tazewell Shepard, Kennedy's naval aide, is among those who meet Air Force One at Andrews.

Shepard: "I remember that when we went to meet the plane when it came to Andrews, they didn't have a rollout stairway. I remember I reached up and lifted her (Mrs. Kennedy) down (from the truck lift). I'll never forget the anguish on her face."

Ms. Carpenter disembarks behind the Johnsons.

Ms. Carpenter: "As he (President Johnson) had suggested, (we walked) to the foot of the plane where there was a very disorganized group of people waiting — congressmen, just looking expressionless; members of the Cabinet; all of the members of the diplomatic corps. The president and Mrs. Johnson went over to the ambulance to say goodbye."

5:10 p.m.

Mrs. Kennedy, Robert Kennedy and Brig. Gen. Godfrey McHugh sit in the rear of the Navy ambulance with the coffin. In front are three Secret Service agents and Dr. George G. Burkley, President Kennedy's physician. The ambulance begins the trip to Bethesda Naval Hospital, where an

autopsy will be performed. Johnson walks into a flood of television lights and delivers his brief statement.

Johnson: "This is a sad time for all people. We have suffered a loss that cannot be weighed. For me it is a deep personal tragedy. I know the world shares the sorrow that Mrs. Kennedy and her family bear. I will do my best. That is all I can do. I ask for your help — and God's."

5:11 p.m.

Johnson and his entourage walk to two nearby helicopters for the brief flight to the White House. Joining them aboard are Special Assistant to the President Bundy, Defense Secretary Robert McNamara and Undersecretary of State George Ball.

Ball: "He (Johnson) was recounting the events of the day, and he was very touched that Mrs. Kennedy had refused to change her stockings, which had the president's blood on them. He had been greatly impressed by the stalwart spirit that she had shown throughout the whole affair....

"He asked us for heaven's sake to stay with him. 'You are the three men I trust the most,' and so on. It was an emotional reaction, not a particularly reasoned one. He said, 'I have inherited from Kennedy the finest group of people in the world, and I just hope they stay with me and trust me.'"

5:25 p.m.

The Navy ambulance arrives at Bethesda. Powers and other Kennedy aides follow.

Powers: "The trip took about 15 minutes; I remember going very quickly and with an escort. When we got to Bethesda, Kenny (O'Donnell) and I started making calls to the White House and the Secret Service.

"There was a lot to do and we sat there with Jackie."

5:26 p.m.

The helicopters land on the White House grounds.

Ms. Carpenter: "Again, there was a battery of newspaper people. The Secret Service man motioned to Mrs. Johnson's car in front of the White House, and the president said to me, 'Stay with Lady Bird and help her all you can.'

"I got into the car, and we started driving through the night to The Elms (the vice president's official residence), rolling up the window so we could talk. Both of us were well aware of what dreadful thing had happened and the difficult days ahead — made even more difficult because this had occurred in the home state of the vice president.

"And I said to her, 'It's a terrible thing to say, but the salvation of Texas is that the governor was hit.'

"And she said, 'Don't think I haven't thought of that. I only wish it could have been me.'"

Valenti is among those who accompany Johnson after their landing on the south grounds of the White House.

Valenti: "I followed the president and everyone else...down the steps that lead you to the basement of the White House...and across Executive Avenue into the EOB (Executive Office Building, where Johnson had his vice presidential office).

"He did not even stop in the president's office....

"I remember that night congressional leaders came. I remember Sen. (Everett M.) Dirksen came and the speaker (John McCormack) and others to be ushered in to see the president."

6:20 p.m.

On White House stationery, Johnson writes letters to Kennedy's 2-year-old son, John Jr., and 5-year-old daughter, Caroline.

The Elms (shown in a 1975 photo), where President Johnson returned.

To John: "It will be many years before you understand fully what a great man your father was. His loss is a deep personal tragedy for all of us, but I wanted you particularly to know that I share your grief. You can always be proud of him."

To Caroline: "Your father's death has been a great tragedy for the nation, as well as for you, and I wanted you to know how much my thoughts are of you at this time."

7:10 p.m.

In Dallas, Oswald is charged with Tippit's murder. For security reasons, he is arraigned in Capt. Fritz's office.

Assistant District Attorney Alexander: "To prevent the filing of a writ of habeas corpus, we decided we would file on him real quick. There wasn't a whole lot of concern about civil rights at that time, but we wanted to go ahead and file.

"I'd taken a little packet of complaints up there (to Fritz's office) with me. I filed on Oswald for shooting Tippit....Justice of the Peace Johnston told him (Oswald) he'd been charged with the murder of officer Tippit. He (Oswald) said, 'This is not a court. You can't get arraigned here.'

"About 40 people were peeking through the blinds."

8 p.m.

Powers is among those who wait with Mrs. Kennedy as the autopsy is performed at Bethesda. George Thomas, Kennedy's valet, arrives with several suits and ties.

Powers: "We picked out clothes for the president...a blue suit — it was his favorite, he called it his 'TV suit' — a white shirt and a solid blue tie....

"At that time, we were not certain if the coffin was going to be open. I had told Bobby and Jackie earlier in the evening that politicians have to go to a lot of wakes, especially an Irish politician, and Jack did not enjoy them....He told me he didn't want anyone looking down at him and deciding whether he looked good or bad, or like he was sleeping."

8:27 p.m.

Johnson tells Valenti, who has been working in an outer office, that he is ready to go home to The Elms.

Valenti: "(He) came out of his office and called me to the side and said to me, 'You can go home with me and you can stay at The Elms.' I said, 'Yes, sir.'...

"There was a great blur of activity that night. When we got to The Elms...we went into the president's den."

Associated Press

Secretary of State Dean Rusk speaks for Kennedy's Cabinet members after their return to Andrews Air Force Base.

Horace Busby, a longtime Johnson friend, is waiting for Johnson at The Elms.

Busby: "When he came in, Mrs. Johnson was coming down the stairs, and they embraced out in the lobby and spoke, very briefly, holding each other, and then he came on out to this little room....

"There was one thing on the wall, and that was a portrait of Sam Rayburn, who had died in 1961. Johnson came in and...before he did anything else, he looked directly at the portrait and kind of threw a salute to it and said, 'Old friend, how I wish you were here.'

"He turned over to me and said, 'You know, I imagine I know less about what's gone on today than any other person in the United States.'"

11 p.m. to midnight

At Bethesda, the autopsy continues. Mrs. Kennedy, Robert Kennedy and family friends, including O'Brien, talk quietly in a waiting room.

O'Brien: "After a considerable period of time of just sitting around, frankly, or standing around, it dawned on us that the coffin had been marked up, the handle had been broken, and don't ask me what prompts you to do things like this, but...I suggested that Dave (Powers) and Ken (O'Donnell) and I go to the nearest funeral parlor and select a coffin....

"We went down to Gawler's Funeral Parlor and...I remember saying to the man...'Will you show us the simplest coffin in the display of middle-priced coffins?'

"And he pointed it out to us, and we asked him to move it up to the hospital immediately."

Johnson talks in his bedroom with Valenti, Kennedy aide Bill Moyers and Johnson aide Carter.

Valenti: "I sat in a little chair next to the phone, to the left of his bed. Bill sat on the edge of the bed, and Cliff had a chair in between us. We had the television set on, and the president put on his pajamas, propped himself up in the bed, and we watched the news reports. From time to time he would say, 'Now tomorrow I want to talk to so-and-so.'"

11:25 p.m.

Fritz files a complaint with Justice of the Peace Johnston accusing Oswald of murdering Kennedy. Wade, concerned about reports that Oswald would be charged as part of a conspiracy, goes to the police station.

Wade: "It had gone out over the air that we'd filed on him (Oswald) as part of a Communist conspiracy. Everything you allege in an indictment you have to prove....

"I went down to the police station and found out they had just filed on him for the murder of John F. Kennedy. It didn't allege any Communist conspiracy or anything."

11:31 p.m.

Secretary of State Rusk and other Kennedy Cabinet members land at Andrews Air Force Base. Rusk steps to the microphones where President Johnson had stood earlier that evening.

Rusk: "Those of us who had the honor of serving President Kennedy value the gallantry and wisdom he brought to the grave, awesome and lonely office of the presidency. President Johnson needs and deserves our fullest support."

NOV. 23
SATURDAY

Shortly after midnight

At Dallas police headquarters, police escort Oswald past more than 100 reporters to another room. Jack Ruby is among those in the crowd.

Wade: "It was a mad scene....You had five reporters there from behind the Iron Curtain and people from Europe and from all over the United States. They were yelling: 'Did they beat him up?' or 'Is it police brutality?'

"The chief of police and Fritz and the FBI came up and wanted to know if it was all right if they put him in the show-up room and let them see him.

"That's when I said, 'Take him out there and let them see him. Let them know that he ain't dead.'

"They put him in a show-up room somewhere downstairs. It was just pandemonium....I think they were trying to (ask questions), but...they were behind the screen. He can't see out and they can see in....

"He told the press he wasn't guilty of anything."

Oswald is taken out of the room, and reporters question Wade.

Wade: "Somebody (asked)...was he (Oswald) a Communist?...And I said, 'Well, now, I don't know about that but they found some literature...dealing with Free Cuba Movement.'...I looked up and Jack Ruby is in the audience, and he said, 'No, it is the Fair Play for Cuba Committee.'

"Ruby ran up to me and he said, 'Hi Henry'...real loud...and put his hand to shake hands with me, and I shook hands with him. And he said, 'Don't you know me?' And I am trying to figure out whether I did or not. And he said, 'I am Jack Ruby, I run the Vegas Club.' And I said, 'What are you doing in here?'...

"He said, 'I know all these fellows.'"

About 12:30 a.m.

Investigators are uncertain whether the assassination was the result of a conspiracy, and in the search for others who might have been involved, they focus on Joe Molina, a credit manager at the Texas School Book Depository.

Because he is a member of the American GI Forum, an organization of Hispanic veterans, Molina is listed in Dallas Police Department files as a possible subversive.

Capt. W.P. Gannaway, Assistant District Attorney Alexander and several other police officers go to Molina's home.

Molina: "He (Gannaway) said, 'Well, what do you know about this fellow Oswald?' I said, 'I don't know anything. He was just a fellow who worked in shipping and I worked in the second floor in the office.'...They said, you had something to do with Oswald so you better tell us because if you don't, it's gonna go bad for you....My response was still the same. I didn't know anything. They had it all wrong."

The police display a search warrant.

A Marine drill team marches in front of the ambulance carrying Kennedy's coffin as the procession enters the White House gates.

Military honor guards keep watch over Kennedy's coffin, which rests on a catafalque in the center of the East Room at the White House.

UPI/Bettmann Newsphotos

Molina: "They went through all the rooms in the house....They would ask questions about Oswald. If I was involved in any subversive activities. I would tell them no....

"They opened a drawer and took out a letter addressed to my wife. The letter was from a friend in Laredo. They had baptized one of their daughters. In the Mexican-American tradition, when you are a godfather or godmother, men called themselves *compadres* and women call themselves *comadres*. When they saw this, they tried to associate it with Dear Comrade, and they jumped on that and said they wanted to keep that letter.

"They looked through every page of the children's schoolbooks and went into the bathroom and even took my wife's Kotex out of the box and split them in half."

The police tell Molina to report to the homicide office for questioning later in the morning.

1:30 a.m.

Oswald is arraigned on a charge of murdering Kennedy.

About 2 a.m.

In Washington, Busby sits in a chair in the Johnsons' bedroom.

Busby: "Mrs. Johnson put on her eye shade to blot out the light. She was going to try to sleep. We kept talking and she raised her eye shade and she said, 'Well, at least this is only for five months.' She counted on her fingers. She was counting up to the convention (the next summer). I guess she was assuming it would all end by the convention.

"And I said, 'No, Mrs. Johnson, it's more likely five years, if not nine years.' And she looked at me — oh, she was angry. She said, 'Don't you say that.'

"He (Johnson) acted like he was a little shocked by her intensity, and he patted her and he said, 'Now honey, Buz is right, at least it's going to five years,' and she didn't like that, and snapped that eye shade back and went down under the covers.

"And he finally turned out the light....I thought from his breathing that he was asleep, so I got up and started around the bed and got to the door and he wasn't asleep. 'Buz.' So I came back and sat down. I did that about three times. He just wanted somebody there."

2:30 a.m.

Aides leave Johnson's bedroom.

Valenti: "We let him go to sleep, and all of us spent the night."

About 3 a.m.

Preparations are made for the arrival of Kennedy's body at the White House. Lt. Col. Paul Miller, director of ceremonies and special events for the Military District of Washington, talks to Kennedy's brother-in-law, Sargent Shriver.

Miller: "I took Shriver out to show him, run through a little rehearsal of what would happen when the president's body arrived from Bethesda. He said, 'Well, Miller, we ought to have some troops meet him at the entrance to the White House and escort him in.'

"(Naval aide Tazewell) Shepard...called the Marine barracks and...told them to provide a detail in dress uniform ASAP. Seventeen minutes later the detail arrived at the southwest gate of the White House, double-timed up the driveway onto the North Lawn all dressed and ready to go."

In Dallas, Jack Ruby has just left the Dallas Times Herald, where he spoke with a printer about changing an ad to show that his clubs would be closed for the weekend.

He is upset about a black-bordered ad titled "Welcome Mr. Kennedy" published in The Dallas Morning News *Nov. 22. The ad, signed by Bernard Weissman of the American Fact-Finding Committee, is critical of Kennedy, and Ruby believes the black border was an implied death threat. Ruby also is upset about a billboard on North Central Expressway that reads, "Impeach Earl Warren."*

UPI/Bettmann Newsphotos

President Lyndon Johnson leaves his home on a rainy Saturday morning, heading for his office in the Executive Office Building and a full day of meetings.

He goes to his Oak Cliff apartment and awakens George Senator, a postcard salesman who has shared the apartment for about three weeks.

Senator: "He said to me, 'Why did it have to happen to a lovely family like that?' and he felt very sorry for Mrs. Kennedy and her children. He got me out of bed."

Ruby: "I…very impatiently awakened George Senator… 'You will have to get up, George. I want you to go with me.'

"I called the club and I asked this kid, Larry (Crafard), if he knew how to pack a Polaroid, and he said, 'Yes.' And I said, 'Get up.' And we went down and picked up Larry."

Ruby wants to take a picture of the "Impeach Earl Warren" billboard, which he thinks may list the same post office box number as the Morning News *ad.*

Ruby: "There was a similar (post office box) number…but I thought at the time it would be the same number of 1792 (the number listed on the Weissman ad), but it was 1757. That is the reason I went down there, to take the Polaroid picture of it….

"I went to the post office to check on box 1792. I even inquired with the man in charge of where you purchase the boxes, and I said to him, 'Who bought this box?' And he said, 'I can't give you the information. All I know is, it is a legitimate business box purchase.'"

3:34 a.m.

The ambulance drives up to the White House, escorted by the Marines. A standard team of six body bearers, under the direction of Army Lt. Sam Bird, unloads the coffin and struggles up the portico steps, realizing that the coffin is far heavier than anticipated. The body bearers include Army Sgt. James Felder.

Felder: "We barely got it in the White House. That's when I told Lieutenant Bird, we're going to have to add two more men (to the team); we'll never get it up the steps of the Capitol. So we picked another Marine and another sailor."

Associated Press

Rose Kennedy enters St. Francis Xavier Church in Hyannis, Mass., for a memorial Mass for her son.

An honor guard made up of members of each of the military services is present to stand watch at the four corners of the coffin as well as at the door on arrival. George Perrault, a Navy petty officer second class, is stationed by the door as the family enters. Also present is Joseph Hagan, operations manager of Gawler's funeral home.

Perrault: "I really have memories of Mrs. Kennedy coming in with her pink dress still with bloodstains on her legs and dress. Even though we were supposed to look straight forward, I let my eyes roam a little bit."

Hagan: "Something like that is beyond description — the reverence, the respect, the elegance of the room itself.

Then, after a while, they brought Mrs. Kennedy down and the coffin was opened. There were a few moments of just, strictly, silence."

About 3:40 a.m.

A priest says a brief blessing. Among those present is Pierre Salinger, the White House press secretary.

Salinger: "Jackie had arranged for a short religious ceremony in the East Room for the White House staff. After the ceremony ended, she came and put her arm around me. She said, 'I know what kind of a day you've had. Why don't you sleep here tonight?' She also

asked Larry O'Brien and Kenny O'Donnell to spend the night."

O'Brien: "Those couple of nights we stayed in the White House I remember having nightmares, having trouble sleeping. I was trying to convince myself that this was a nightmare."

About 4 a.m.

In Chicago, officials at Klein's Sporting Goods find an American Rifleman *coupon used to order a 6.5mm Mannlicher-Carcano rifle eight months before — the same type of gun that police suspect was the weapon used to kill Kennedy. The coupon is addressed to A. Hidell at a Dallas post office box; later Saturday, FBI handwriting experts say the writing on the coupon is Oswald's.*

In Washington, Kennedy's aides discuss whether to have an open coffin.

O'Brien: "Bobby Kennedy spoke to Ken O'Donnell and I....He suggested to us that we make that decision. So we went into the East Room, where the coffin was closed, and there were servicemen at each corner of the coffin, and our decision was not to open the coffin."

5:50 a.m.

Dawn comes to Washington. It is a gray, rainy day.

Shepard: "It just seems to me that the heavens were crying."

6 a.m.

The phone is ringing in Salinger's room in the West Wing of the White House.

Salinger: "The White House operator said, 'Mr. Salinger, the president wants to talk to you.' Immediately the thought ran through my mind that I had had a terrible nightmare. Then a voice said, 'Pierre, this is Lyndon.' It struck home probably even more that Kennedy was really dead...."

"He told me how sorry he was about John Kennedy being killed. I said I knew he'd be able to adopt the problems of the country, but I was resigning as press secretary. He said, 'You can't resign, I need you for the transition.'"

Starting early Saturday, officials grapple with the details of the funeral, the transition to the new administration — even the question of whether football games should be held on Sunday.

Salinger: "I had graduated from college with Pete Rozelle, and by this time he was commissioner of the NFL. He called me at the White House and asked if he should cancel the games on Sunday. I told him that if he'd asked that question of President Kennedy, he'd never have told him to cancel the games."

In Hyannis, Mass., Rose Kennedy goes to Mass at St. Francis Xavier.

About 7 a.m.

At Parkland, assistant administrator Landregan arrives for work.

Landregan: "By Saturday morning we were moving the state capital into Parkland. The governor was still in intensive care, but it was obvious he was going to be all right....The governor appeared worn but was talking and seemed quite lucid....

"I got to the hospital shortly before 7 o'clock; one of the first things I did was to go to my desk to get a razor and shaving cream for the governor. We had fabricated a shield to put in front of the window in the room where the governor was going to be moved. This shield was made of steel or something like that, and it was intended to deflect a bullet. We still did not know if this had been part of a conspiracy or what."

In Washington, the last telegrams of invitation are sent to relatives and close Kennedy acquaintances for a morning

Mass in the East Room. Also, Yarborough, like other government officials and workers throughout the nation, prepares himself and his staff for the new leadership.

Yarborough: "I remember going to my office to call my chief of staff and others and have them come to the office....I told them, our whole relationship with the White House has changed. It's a whole different world...a different kind of government. Kennedy and I were close friends....I was not close with Johnson. He'd tried to keep me out of the Senate (in 1957)....

"I told them...the situation worldwide has changed. Kennedy intended to settle the war in Vietnam and get out as soon as the '64 election was over. I didn't think Johnson would do that. I told them we will not have close friends in charge anymore. Things had changed — not just personalities but policies."

8 a.m.

Although it has not yet been decided whether to hold the funeral in Massachusetts or the Washington area, Robert McNamara travels to Arlington National Cemetery to inspect possible burial sites after conferring with John Metzler, superintendent of Arlington. Accompanying McNamara are Gen. Maxwell Taylor, chairman of the Joint Chiefs of Staff, and Army Secretary Cyrus Vance.

At Hyannis Port, family members and friends decide it is time to tell John Kennedy's ailing father, Joseph, of his son's death. Ted Kennedy, sitting at his bedside, delivers the news.

After 8:30 a.m.

Ruby is at his apartment watching a memorial service in New York on television.

Ruby: "I watched Rabbi Seligman....He eulogized that here is a man (Kennedy) that fought in every battle, went to every country, and had to come

back to his own country to be shot in the back.

"That created a tremendous emotional feeling for me, the way he said that."

About 9 a.m.

The Rev. John Cavanaugh celebrates Mass in the East Room for the Kennedy family and friends.

Powers: "It was raining in Washington that day, and I just kept looking out the window. The weather fit the mood of what was happening inside. The rain was beating against the White House, and the White House had always looked so beautiful before to me....That day, it just was draped in black."

In Dallas, flowers and other memorials to Kennedy start appearing on the grassy knoll. Roslyn Carren, owner of Carren's Flowers on Lovers Lane, handles one of the special requests.

Mrs. Carren: "We opened Saturday morning and the note was under the door — no name, handwritten on a piece of blue-lined white paper just ripped off of something. And there were two $20 bills and a 10 (in the envelope). I remember that because it was very impressive to us. At that time, a big wreath would be 10, 15 dollars.

"The note specifically asked for all white flowers....It (the wreath) was large and it was on an easel. Alvin (Cooper, the delivery man) brought it down and stuck it into the ground....They didn't instruct him where to place it, just down there at the (assassination) site."

Preparations begin for the burial of officer Tippit. The Rev. C.D. Tipps, pastor of the Beckley Hills Baptist Church, who will officiate at the funeral, sees Tippit's widow, Marie, who is a member of the church.

Tipps: "She was a lady who was utterly dependent on him. On Saturday I read Scripture to her and prayed with

Ethel Kennedy arrives at the White House to view the coffin.

Former President Dwight Eisenhower confers with President Johnson.

her. I tried to get her to see that that wasn't all of it, that life didn't have to end there."

9:40 a.m.

After the East Room Mass, Mrs. Kennedy goes to gaze at the just-redecorated West Wing rooms. Already Kennedy's possessions are being packed into cartons. Meanwhile, government officials, family members, diplomats and others come to pay their respects to Kennedy in the East Room.

State Department Chief of Protocol Angier Duke: "Lincoln had lain in state in the East Room, and she (Mrs. Kennedy) chose that, I think, with much the same decoration, the hanging of the black curtains from the windows. All of that was done from pictures and drawings and renditions of Lincoln lying there.

"It was very impressive, very awesome, in a very majestic way."

McNamara returns to Arlington National Cemetery with Robert Kennedy and oth-

ers for further discussion of a possible grave site. Among those present is Bernard G. Carroll, a lieutenant colonel in the Army and post engineer at Fort Myers. The sentiment begins to shift in favor of an Arlington burial.

Carroll: "Secretary McNamara and a group from the Pentagon came over and, with the Kennedys, decided where the grave would be....They picked a site that was in line with the center of the Lincoln Memorial and the center of the Lincoln Bridge and the Lee Custis Mansion that sits on the hill above the grave. It had to be on the center line of those three things. We took a surveying instrument and lined it up."

About 10 a.m.

A small memorial service for Kennedy is held at Parkland Memorial Hospital. Lee Lindsley, pastor of Greenville Avenue Christian Church and chaplain at the Dallas County Jail, speaks at the service.

Lindsley: "The governor's brother and sister-in-law were among those in atten-

dance. It was on the first floor in a little chapel they had there. Chaplain (Kenneth) Pepper and I spoke. The whole thing lasted maybe 12, 15 minutes.

"On Saturday the whole city was in shock. Everyone was walking around numb. You'd drive down the street and see people walking, with their eyes to the ground."

Mourners also gather at churches across the city to pray. The Rev. Thomas Keithley, assistant to the dean at St. Matthew's (Episcopal) Cathedral, goes to Sacred Heart Cathedral.

Keithley: "I went...to say prayers there for Kennedy. I felt somehow I ought to, that I would go there because President Kennedy was Roman Catholic. There were quite a few people at that time, not an organized service being led, but there were just quite a few people just coming and going or kneeling...saying their prayers or the rosary.

"There was that kind of feeling (antagonism toward Catholics) and that might have made a difference subconsciously to me, that those of us who were not Roman Catholics should make a witness to the fact that whether we had voted for Kennedy or not was irrelevant.

"He was elected and installed as our president and this was a great tragedy for the nation, and you have to uphold the office of president, too."

10:05 a.m.

The President and Mrs. Johnson go to the East Room to view Kennedy's body.

Mrs. Johnson: "Lyndon walked slowly past the president's body in the East Room....At one end was a Catholic image, I don't know quite what it was. It wasn't just a cross, but more elaborate....

"I was reminded, caught up in the thought, that the Catholic faith has a pattern for everything — a pattern for life, and a pattern for death....

"An air of quiet prevailed, an utter, complete quiet that seemed to grip — well, the whole country, I suppose."

About 10:25 a.m.

The Dallas Police Department is a flurry of activity throughout the morning, as District Attorney Wade tries to find a lawyer to represent Oswald, Molina arrives for questioning and another search of Ruth Paine's home in Irving is ordered.

Oswald is questioned by homicide Capt. Fritz. Also present is Secret Service Agent Forrest Sorrels.

Fritz: "I asked him if he belonged to the Communist Party....He said he did not. He said he never had a card. He told me again that he did belong to the Fair Play for Cuba organization, that he was in favor of the Castro revolution.

"I asked him what he thought of the president....He said he didn't have any particular comment to make about the president. He said he had a nice family, that he admired his family....At one time I told him, I said, 'You know you have killed the president, and this is a very serious charge.'

Authorities confer at the Dallas Police Department; the questioning of Oswald continues, as do efforts to find an attorney for him.

"He denied it and said he hadn't killed the president....I said he had been killed. He said people will forget that within a few days and there would be another president."

Sorrels: "He was questioned about the rifle, because at that time, as I recall it, it had been determined that the rifle had been purchased from Klein's in Chicago and shipped to a person using the name of A. Hidell....

"He denied that the rifle was his. He denied knowing or using the name of A. Hidell, or Alek Hidell....He still maintained an arrogant, defiant attitude....He gave me the impression of

lying to Captain Fritz and deliberately doing so."

Wade tries to find someone to represent Oswald, who has requested assistance from New York lawyer John Abt.

Wade: "I tried to get ahold of John Abt Saturday morning, and finally one of my assistants got ahold of him or talked to him. He said he was not going to handle the case, was not interested in it.

"I got the president of the Dallas Bar and the president of the Dallas Criminal Bar to go down and see him. They

UPI/Bettmann Newsphotos

President Kennedy's rocking chair is wheeled from the White House as the family's belongings are moved.

reported he (Oswald) said he didn't want them."

Homicide detective Rose obtains a search warrant and returns to the Paine home, where Marina Oswald has been staying and where Oswald visited on weekends.

Rose: "We searched the house and we did bring in a great deal of property that belonged to Oswald. He had stored it there in the Paine garage....

"I found a photograph of the back of a house, a large house and we were able to later identify that house as (retired Maj. Gen. Edwin) Walker's home. The

significant thing there is, months before the assassination someone tried to kill General Walker....

"The second significant thing was, I found the photograph and the negative of Oswald holding the rifle, wearing the pistol on his hip, holding the newspaper in his hand....

"He had copies of some letters where he had written to Gus Hall, Communist Party secretary in the United States. He had copies of letters he had written to the State Department when he was in Russia, wanting to come back home. He had copies of some leaflets he had had printed up called Fair Play for Cuba Committee."

10:30 a.m.

In Washington, Johnson meets with former President Dwight Eisenhower, one of many briefings and conferences he holds throughout the day.

Johnson aide Busby: "He (Eisenhower) had a lot of suggestions...about people he thought he (Johnson) should call, that sort of thing, very good suggestions."

Johnson aide Valenti: "He (Eisenhower) was somber-faced and unsmiling. He said he was very grateful for the president calling him, and was delighted he could come in and talk....

"Later, Johnson said to me that Eisenhower was solid, which to Johnson was a pretty high accolade."

About 11:30 a.m.

Busby, waiting for Johnson in a reception area in the Old Executive Office Building, is directed to a small, sparsely furnished room he has never visited before.

Busby: "There sat Lyndon Johnson at the desk, and at the table was Walter Jenkins, his principal assistant. I came in and was standing up, and Johnson used his hand in kind of a little waving sign, gesturing for me to bend over.

"Those windows...looked out over the west entrance to the White House, and he did not want anybody outside to be able to look up and see anybody look out those windows at the White House. He didn't want to be seen himself looking at the White House like he was anxious to get over there. It turned out we were all hunched over all day."

About noon

Oswald's wife, Marina, and mother, Marguerite Oswald, go to the Dallas County Courthouse.

Marguerite Oswald: "We waited quite a while. One of the men came by and said, 'I am sorry that we are going to be delayed in letting you see Lee, but we have picked up another suspect.'

"I said to Marina, 'Oh, Marina, good, another man they think maybe shot Kennedy.'"

School Book Depository employee Joe Molina, the "'second man," has been waiting at police headquarters all morning to be questioned again.

Molina: "There was havoc there, reporters everywhere, cameras everywhere....They put me in a waiting room. They were questioning Oswald at the time....Finally I asked if they were going to talk to me or not....

"Maybe an hour later they took me to another room, where I was questioned by (Dallas police Lt.) Jack Revill. He started asking me about the American GI Forum, what kind of an organization was it.

"So I explained to him...(it) was a veterans organization with its makeup being mostly Mexican-Americans. He kept asking me about the forum and did I know there were some Communist members....I said no....He insisted we had Communist affiliations and I insisted there were none....

"In the meantime, they were giving these television interviews, saying they were questioning a second man and all that, and I wasn't even aware of that."

12:31 p.m.

Kennedy's rocking chairs are removed to the Old Executive Office Building.

1 p.m.

Johnson telephones officer Tippit's widow, Marie, to express his condolences. Mrs. Tippit's brother, Dwight Gasway, also consoles his sister.

Gasway: "It was a very difficult time for the family....Things were pretty much in an uproar. All the kinfolk were coming in and officers who knew him were stopping by all the time."

1:06 p.m.

Mrs. Kennedy goes to Arlington National Cemetery to make a final decision on her husband's grave site. She sees the site selected earlier by McNamara and others.

Cemetery superintendent Metzler: "She said, 'This is perfect.'...She said, 'This is exactly the way he (Kennedy) described it.' Apparently he had come over a couple of weeks earlier with John-John and he said, 'This is the most perfect view of Washington. I could stay here forever.'"

Throughout the afternoon, Mrs. Kennedy continues to make funeral arrangements. Among those involved is Miller, the military district's director of ceremonies and special events.

Miller: "The procedure was as outlined in the state funeral plan. She had requested participation of the Black Watch (a Scottish bagpipe group), and she requested participation of the Special Forces and the Irish cadets...the Irish equivalent of our military academy, I believe. She requested participation of the 3rd Infantry's fife and drum corps and the Air Force pipe band. So they were worked into the funeral proceedings in a proper way."

Plans are also made to have Air Force One join a planned flyby of Air Force and Navy jets over the grave despite some concern that the big plane will spook the horses in the program. Col. Swindal, pilot of Air Force One, knows how much the plane meant to Kennedy and is pleased to learn of the flyby.

Swindal: "We were glad to hear it because we...wanted to do something like that."

About 1:10 p.m.

Marina and Marguerite Oswald are allowed to talk to Oswald by telephone in a visitor's booth at the city jail.

Marguerite Oswald: "Lee seemed very severely composed and assured. He was well beaten up. He had black eyes and his face was all bruised and everything. But he was very calm.

"He smiled with his wife, and talked with her, and then I got on the phone and I said, 'Honey, you are so bruised up, your face. What are they doing?' He said, 'Mother, don't worry. I got that in a scuffle.'

"I talked and said, 'Is there anything I can do to help you?' He said, 'No, Mother, everything is fine. I know my rights, and I will have an attorney. I have already requested to get in touch with attorney Abt, I think is the name. Don't worry about a thing.'

"I would say I spent about three or four minutes on the telephone and then Marina came back to the telephone and talked with Lee. So we left. So Marina started crying. Marina says, 'Mama, I tell Lee I love Lee and Lee says he love me very much. And Lee tell me to make sure I buy shoes for June.'"

Marina Oswald: "He tried to console me that I should not worry, that everything would turn out well. He asked about how the children were. He spoke of some friends who supposedly would help him. I don't know who he had in mind. That he had written to someone in New York before that....

"I told him that the police had been there and that a search had been conducted, that they had asked me whether we had a rifle, and I had answered yes. And he said that if there would be a trial, and that if I am questioned, it would be my right to answer or to refuse to answer.

"I said, 'I don't believe that you did that (killed Tippit), and everything will turn out well.' I couldn't accuse him — after all, he was my husband.

"He said that I should not worry, that everything would turn out well. But I could see by his eyes that he was guilty. Rather he tried to appear to be brave. However, by his eyes I could tell that he was afraid."

The Dallas Morning News

A visitor writes a message beside one of the many floral arrangements placed by mourners near the Texas School Book Depository.

1:30 p.m.

Johnson holds his first Cabinet meeting, which lasts 25 minutes. The president opens with a silent prayer and then asks for the advisers' guidance and support. Robert Kennedy arrives late. George Reedy, special assistant to Johnson, is among the non-Cabinet officials attending.

Reedy: "The mood was uneasy. Nobody quite knew where to go.... Everybody was there, all of the Kennedy people and all of us, and it was rather interesting....

"I remember Adlai Stevenson as the senior officer — he was ambassador to the United Nations — saying to the president that obviously everybody there was at his service and pledged to serve him loyally and completely....

"One of his (Johnson's) goals at that particular moment was to convince the American people that a crackpot with a mail-order rifle couldn't kill the United States. If you kill a president, somebody else steps into his place and carries on. And he very much wanted to carry on the Kennedy policies.

"Therefore he was sort of looking to the Kennedy staff members for clues as to what Kennedy had wanted done. And I think they were looking to him for clues as to what he wanted done. Nobody quite knew where to go."

About 2 p.m.

In Dallas, wreaths and other memorials continue to be laid at the grassy knoll. Alvin Cooper, delivery man for Carren's Flowers, takes a large wreath to the area.

Cooper: "There were a lot of people down there, just milling around. There was a few sobs and people with cameras. It was awfully crowded that day....At the end of the day, I think that thing was practically full of flowers....

"It felt rather strange. It was like something that was out of the ordinary, like it wasn't real....

"The people that were gathered, I think they were whispering to each other...'It's a sad thing' or 'Isn't that a shame?' or something like that."

Jonsson, president of the Dallas Citizens Council, consults with city leaders about how Dallas should respond to the assassination.

Jonsson: "My telephone never stopped ringing. My home became a retreat for us to get people together. We were trying to determine what we should do next to show the Kennedy family we, too, were desolate and grieved about what had happened to the president.

"It was agreed that four of us would go to Washington. That we would go to the Mayflower Hotel where the Chamber of Commerce had set up an office (for congressional lobbying).

"The Dallas representative there was well-known and knew how to get around and knew some of the Kennedy people. We thought it important that they knew we had thought enough to go out there."

About 3 p.m.

Wes Wise, a sportscaster-reporter for KRLD-TV, pulls over across the street from the Texas School Book Depository.

Wise: "Out of the corner of my eye I saw a guy kind of running, kind of walking fast....He said, 'Wes! Wes!' and I turned around (and) it was Jack Ruby.

"He was probably dressed in exactly the same clothes he was dressed in the next morning because it met that description exactly — a blue suit and a fedora-type hat. He says, 'Isn't this awful. Isn't this awful.' And I said, 'Yeah, it sure is, Jack.'...

"He says, 'I just can't imagine how awful it will be for Jackie Kennedy to be asked to come back here to testify as a witness on the murder of her husband.'

"I said I was out at the Trade Mart when it happened....I told him how people were in a state of shock, and I said I was shown the Western saddles that were to be given John-John and Caroline.

"And tears came to his eyes and he says, 'Oh' — kind of a little bit of a sob but definitely tears in his eyes. He says, 'Oh, oh, that's awful, oh, that's terrible. I just can't imagine what anguish that will cause those children.'"

After 3 p.m.

District Attorney Wade continues his work on the Oswald case.

Wade: "They had sent that rifle up to the FBI to examine it....They were trying to compare bullets and also, according to the Dallas policeman, there was a palm print on there that matched his (Oswald's)....I don't think the FBI even-

tually confirmed that....But they didn't say it wasn't his print and didn't say it was.

"I went down and talked to the people at the Police Department....They said they would have him (Oswald) available for me to interview, but I said this is no place....They said they were going to move him and I said, 'I'll see him at 2 o'clock after you get him in the county jail on Sunday.'

"I did ask him (Police Chief Jesse Curry) not to discuss the thing because it had already had so much publicity that it was going to be difficult to try him here."

3:30 p.m.

Robert Oswald speaks to his brother Lee at the jail.

Robert Oswald: "I did try to point out to him that the evidence was overwhelming that he did kill police officer Tippit and possibly the president. To this he replied, 'Do not form any opinion on the so-called evidence.'"

Ruby has been driving throughout the downtown area talking to people about the assassination.

Ruby: "We went over to the Turf Bar Lounge, and it was a whole hullabaloo, and I showed the pictures (of) 'Impeach Earl Warren' to (Dallas jeweler Frank) Bellochio, and he saw the picture and got very emotional.

"And Bellochio said, 'Why did the newspaper take this ad of Weissman?' And Bellochio said, 'I have got to leave Dallas.'...

"Suddenly you realize if you love the city, you stay here and you make the best of it. I said, 'The city was good enough for you all before this. Now you feel that way about it.'"

After 4 p.m.

The police drive Molina, the "second man," home.

Molina: "My wife was very much upset. She said all these reports, although they didn't mention my name, said there was a second man, implications that I was associated with Oswald in some manner. I tried to reassure her there was nothing....

"My feeling was that I was just an innocent individual caught in the hysteria and I was trying to keep as calm as I could, where, believe me, that was hard to do."

Police do not question Molina again. Later, Warren Commission attorneys assure him that he is not suspected of any involvement in the assassination.

About 6:30 p.m.

The questioning of Oswald resumes. Detective Rose has returned from the search of the Paine residence and has given Fritz the photograph showing Oswald carrying a rifle and wearing a pistol on his hip.

Rose: "I brought the photograph to Captain Fritz and showed it to him....Later we were able to show that was the same rifle that was found on the sixth floor of the book depository....

"Captain Fritz said (to Oswald) after some preliminary talk...'You told me you'd never owned a rifle in your life.' And he said, 'That's right. I never did.' 'Never owned a pistol?' 'No, sir. Never owned a pistol in my life,' he said.

"Captain Fritz showed him the picture and said, 'Let me show you this and tell me whose rifle is this.' Well, when he showed it to him, Oswald was visibly upset. It made him mad....

"And he said, 'Well, that's not me. Somebody has superimposed my face over that body.' Captain Fritz said, 'It is your face, though.'

"And he (Oswald) snapped. . .'No, on second look, it's not even my face. It's somebody just kind of resembles me.'"

7:15 p.m.

Oswald is returned to his cell.

9:40 p.m.

The Johnsons have dinner with friends at The Elms. Busby arrives about 40 minutes after dinner to talk to Johnson.

Busby: "He left the dinner and came out to talk to me, and told me about talking to the Kennedy people that day, and he was real pleased that they had agreed to stay on."

At the White House, relatives and close friends gather for dinner. Afterward, several again visit the East Room. Mrs. Kennedy asks Senate Majority Leader Mike Mansfield to speak at the Capitol Rotunda on Sunday after the coffin is moved there, and he agrees.

In Dallas, reporters and photographers gather at the Police Department to await further developments with Oswald.

Police Chief Jesse Curry: "They (reporters) said, 'Are you going to transfer him tonight?' and I said, 'No, we are not going to transfer him tonight.' I said, 'We are tired. We are going home and get some rest.'

"Something was said (by one of the reporters) about 'Well, we are tired, too. When should we come back?' And...I told them, 'If you are back here by 10 o'clock in the morning, I don't think that you would miss anything you want to see.'"

11:44 p.m.

Breck Wall (real name: Billy Ray Wilson), an entertainer and friend of Ruby's, is at his parents' home in Galveston. Ruby telephones him.

Wall: "He was like really, really angry. Abe Weinstein had the Colony Club next door to his and he was very, very upset that Abe had stayed open....He (Ruby) was ranting, raving mad.

"I was the head of AGVA, which was the entertainers' union....I think originally when he called me he was asking if there was anything I could do to make him (Weinstein) shut down.

"Then in the course of the conversation he started talking about Oswald. I don't think he ever said his name. He said, 'This guy who killed our president, someone needs to do the same to him.'"

About midnight

Ruby has just left the Carousel Club after making a series of phone calls. He drops by a friend's McKinney Avenue club.

Ruby: "I didn't do anything but visit a little club over here and had a Coca-Cola, because I was sort of depressed. A fellow that owns the Pago Club, Bob Norton, knew something was wrong with me in the certain mood I was in."

NOV. 24

SUNDAY

After midnight

Oswald's impending transfer from the city jail to the Dallas County Jail is under discussion at the Police Department.

Detective Rose: "Fritz told us that he had met with the chief (Curry) and the city manager (Elgin Crull) and he was going to have to transfer Oswald publicly for a media event....He was really adamant about it. He was visibly upset. In fact, he told us he was upset."

About 3:20 a.m.

FBI agent Milton Newsom calls Dallas police Capt. W.B. Frazier to inform him of an anonymous threat received at the Dallas FBI office earlier in the morning.

Frazier: "He said he had received a threat from some man to the effect that a group of men, I believe he indicated they had 100 or 200…were going to attempt to kill Oswald that day sometime."

Frazier calls Capt. Fritz.

Fritz: "Captain Frazier…told me they had some threats and he had to transfer Oswald. And I said, 'Well, I don't know.…You had better call (Curry).'… He called me back then in a few minutes and he told me he couldn't get the chief and told me to leave him where he was.

"I don't think that transferring him at night would have been any safer than transferring him during the day. I have always felt that that was Ruby who made that call. I may be wrong. But he was out late that night.…If two or three of those officers had started out with him,

People waiting for a glimpse of Lee Harvey Oswald line Houston Street across from the Dallas County criminal courts building, which houses the county jail, awaiting Oswald's transfer from the city jail.

Associated Press

The Dallas Morning News

Dallas Police Chief Jesse Curry in his office at police headquarters.

Warren Commission

A "Closed" sign is posted in the window of Jack Ruby's Carousel Club. He also closed the Vegas Club for the weekend during mourning for Kennedy.

they may have had the same trouble they had the next morning."

7 to 9 a.m.

Police begin preparations for transferring Oswald out of the Police and Courts Building. The basement is cleared, guards are stationed at the ramps leading into the garage, and officers search the area.

Curry: "We felt that if an attempt was made on him, that it would be made by a group of people. One of the threats that had been made during the night was, 'This is a group of 100 and we will take the prisoner before you get him to the county jail,' so we really expected trouble, if we had trouble, from a group of people and not an individual.

"We discussed the possibility of even some detective or some police officer that might be so emotionally aroused that he might try to take some action against the man, and we tried to be sure that the men we put there were emotionally stable men."

Before 9:30 a.m.

James R. Leavelle, a homicide detective, sees Curry on the first floor of City Hall.

Leavelle: "I suggested to the chief that we double-cross the media and take Oswald out on the first floor and put him in a car and take him down to the county jail. I said, 'We can be down there before anybody knows we've even started with him.'

"And he (Curry) said, 'Well, Leavelle, I told the people that I would transfer him and let the television people film it so that they could see that we haven't abused him, mistreated him, beat him up or anything' and said, 'I'm going to keep my word.'"

About 9:30 a.m.

Ruby is at his apartment reading the newspaper when he sees a letter from a Dallas resident to Caroline Kennedy about her father's death.

Ruby: "Alongside that letter on the same sheet of paper was a small com-

ment in the newspaper that — I don't know how it was stated — Mrs. Kennedy may have to come back for the trial of Lee Harvey Oswald.

"That caused me to go like I did.

"I never spoke to anyone about attempting to do anything. No subversive organization gave me any idea. No underworld person made any effort to contact me. It all happened that Sunday morning.

"I wanted to show my love for our faith, being of the Jewish faith....Suddenly the feeling, the emotional feeling came within me that someone owed this debt to our beloved president to save her (Jackie) the ordeal of coming back."

Senator, Ruby's roommate, sees him eat breakfast, read the newspaper and watch memorial services for Kennedy on television.

Senator: "The effect on Jack was, it put him in a worse mood than he was, more solemn than ever, and he had tears in his eyes."

At the Police Department, Fritz tells homicide detectives L.C. Graves and Leavelle

Stripper Karen "Little Lynn" Bennett worked for Ruby.

Associated Press

that they will transfer Oswald. The original plan is to carry him in an armored car. Before then, Leavelle and Graves are asked to take Oswald to Fritz's office for a final interrogation.

Graves: "We were told by several of the people that were supposed to be in charge of security downstairs, they said everything was secure, all we had to do was bring him out and put him in the car, which would be situated right in the driveway, right even with where we walked out.

"We got him (Oswald) down out of the jail and took him to Captain Fritz's office first."

Homicide detective Charles N. "Chuck" Dhority also sees Oswald.

Dhority: "The only time I saw him scared was when we went up to get him out of jail to transfer him…and I told him there had been threats on his life. He seemed to get scared then."

Fritz, postal inspector Harry D. Holmes and Secret Service Agent Thomas Kelley question Oswald in Fritz's office.

Holmes: "There was no formality to the interrogation. One man would question Oswald. Another would interrupt with a different trend of thought.…

"Oswald was quite composed. He answered readily those questions that he wanted to answer. He could cut off just like with a knife anything that he didn't want to answer.

"And those particular things that he didn't want to answer were anything that pertained with the assassination of the president or the shooting of officer Tippit. He flatly denied any knowledge of either.

"He was not particularly obnoxious. He seemed to be intelligent. He seemed to be clear-minded; he seemed to have a good memory, because in questioning him about the (postal) boxes, which I had original applications in front of me, he was pretty accurate.…

"Someone asked him about what his beliefs were…someone referred to his communism, and he said, 'I am not a communist. I am a Marxist.…A communist is a Lenin Marxist, and I am a true Karl Marxist.'

"So, this Secret Service inspector asked, 'What religion are you?'…And he said, 'I have no faith.' And then he said, 'I suppose you mean the Bible.' 'Well,' he said, 'I have read the Bible. It is fair reading but not very interesting. But as a matter of fact, I am a student of philosophy, and I don't consider the Bible as even a reasonable or intelligent philosophy. I don't think much of it.'"

About 10:15 a.m.

Ruby gets a phone call from Karen "Little Lynn" Bennett, a stripper. Ruby has closed his club in mourning and she hasn't been paid. The rent on her Fort Worth apartment is due, and her landlord has threatened to evict her if she doesn't come up with the money by noon.

Miss Bennett: "The rent was $15. I called Jack and asked him to send me $25, and Jack said, 'Well, I'm going downtown'…or 'I have to go down-

town.' But, anyway, he said he was going downtown and he would drop the money off at Western Union for me so I could get it quicker.…

"He sounded as if he had been crying or was crying or was about to cry. You know, like someone that was far away.… When I talked to him, I had to call him back to the phone three times. I asked, 'Jack, are you still there?' because it seemed like he was far away."

Senator: "He sure had a moody look and very faraway look to me. It was a look that I had never seen before on him.…All he said, he said, 'George, I am taking the dog (Sheba, his favorite dachshund) down to the club.'"

Ruby: "I got a call from a little girl — she wanted some money — that worked for me.…So my purpose was to go to the Western Union — my double purpose — but the thought of doing, committing the act wasn't until I left my apartment."

Among those gathered at the police station in anticipation of Oswald's transfer is Ike Pappas, a reporter with WNEW radio in New York.

Pappas: "I was amazed when I listened to Jesse Curry because he was laying out every bit of the detail of moving this prisoner, probably the most notorious prisoner we've had in this century.… I didn't understand that.

"He had all these people from all over the world in there, and international reporters, and he was playing to the crowd.…

"He told us the time and how they were going to take him, and he was a little confused about how they were going to put him in an armored car."

10 to 11 a.m.

As the crowd grows at the police station, thousands of others gather at Dallas-area churches for Sunday morning services. Many of the ministers address the Kennedy assassination, including the Rev. Thomas Fry Jr., pastor of First Presby-

terian Church, and the Rev. William A. Holmes, pastor of Northaven United Methodist Church.

Fry: "I said it was such a shame. We didn't know why it had happened at the time....

"I made a prediction, which came true, that I felt that the things that Kennedy had stood for probably had a better chance of succeeding now that he was gone than if he had stayed alive. Because there would be such emotion in the country that the next president would have a better chance of getting all the things, which Lyndon Johnson did.

"I talked to them about the fact I really felt that whether it had been from Dallas or not, we had created an atmosphere in which it could happen. And that we had to do something about it.

"I wanted to say that the past is the past. We've got to start again....I felt that we as a city and as a country had a responsibility for seeing that things like that didn't happen....We had too long ignored...the conflict within our city and tried to act like it wasn't there, and you can't do that."

Holmes also delivers a sermon critical of Dallas.

Holmes: "President John Kennedy was killed two days ago in Dallas, and the one thing worse than this is that the citizens of Dallas should declare unto the world, 'We take no responsibility for the death of this man.'...There is no city in the United States which in recent months and years has been more acquiescent toward its extremists than Dallas, Texas."

Holmes' sermon will be broadcast two days later on the CBS Evening News. *Because of phone threats, police will advise Holmes and his family to leave their home for a week. But on Sunday, he has a rapt audience.*

Holmes: "It was standing room only, as was true for churches throughout the nation....It was an atmosphere that con-

tained several dimensions: One was a great sense of tragedy and loss and a great sense of unity....Everybody was just devastated....

"We just acquiesced for months prior to that and let our city be taken over, as far as public image was concerned, by a bunch of extreme, reactionary, right-wing people.

"I just felt that if the Christian faith isn't applicable to this kind of event, I can't imagine what it would be applicable to."

10:47 a.m.

In Washington, the last Kennedy White House Mass concludes, as a small group of friends and relatives leaves the East Room.

About 11 a.m.

Parkland officials are notified by hospital controller Bob Struwe that large crowds have gathered to watch Oswald's transfer.

Assistant administrator Landregan: "Struwe noted that there was a possibility of an incident and suggested we might want to alert the emergency room....Mr. (Pete) Geilich (assistant administrator) then proceeded to the emergency room to alert the emergency room and asked them to delay any lunch hours until after the transfer had been effected."

Ruby is driving toward the Western Union office to send money to Miss Bennett.

Ruby: "I drove down Main Street....I started to go down a driveway, but I wanted to go by the wreaths, and I saw them and started to cry again....

"I guess I thought I knew he (Oswald) was going to be moved at 10 o'clock....I took it for granted he had already been moved.

"Then I drove, parked the car across from the Western Union, went into the Western Union, sent the money order."

After 11 a.m.

Oswald is still being questioned in Fritz's office, and impatience grows for the transfer.

Graves: "Time slipped by, of course. And Elgin Crull was city manager at that time and having committed us to transfer him at 10 o'clock, time slipped by 10 o'clock and everybody got nervous. So finally Chief Curry came up and told us that we had to transfer him."

Oswald earlier had expressed concern that he needed some kind of disguise since everyone had seen him in the clothes he was wearing. The officers offer him two old sweaters, one black and one beige.

Graves: "I asked him (Oswald) which one he wanted to wear....He said, 'I believe I'll wear the black one.'...No, as a matter of fact, he put the other one on. It was in better shape. And then he decided 'no, can I wear the black one?' I said, 'I don't care which one you wear.' So he pulled it off and put the black one on....

"We don't know (why Oswald changed) because the black one had a little hole in it.

"We got him sweatered and handcuffed, and we decided we'd ask Captain Fritz if we could give everybody a slip and take him out on the first floor and get a car and go right on to the county (jail) unannounced....He (Fritz) asked Curry, the chief, 'Why don't we do that?'

"And Chief Curry's final words were: 'We cannot do that. We are obligated to the press. We are an hour late already. Let's move him.'"

Leavelle and Graves prepare to escort Oswald from Fritz's office to the basement.

Leavelle: "I jokingly said to him up there as I was handcuffing myself to him, I said, 'Lee, if anybody shoots at you, I hope they're as good a shot as you are' — meaning that I hope they hit him and not me.

"He kinda laughed. He said, 'Oh, you're being melodramatic about it,' or something to that effect. He said, 'There ain't nobody gonna shoot me.'

"I said, 'If they do, you know what to do, don't you?' And he said, 'Captain Fritz told me to follow you.' He said, 'I'll do whatever you do,' and I said, 'In that case, you will be on the floor in a hurry.'"

Fritz speaks to Chief Curry about the plan to carry Oswald in the armored car.

Fritz: "I said, 'Well, I don't like the idea, Chief, of transferring him in a money wagon.' We, of course, didn't know the driver...nor anything about the money wagon, and he said, 'Well, that is all right. Transfer him in your car like you want to, and we will use the money wagon for a decoy.'"

Word of the new plan is telephoned to the basement, along with instructions for a lead car to be moved up from the garage to Commerce Street behind the armored truck, which has been sitting at the top of the Commerce Street ramp.

Because the truck is blocking the Commerce Street exit, Lt. Rio Sam Pierce drives the lead car out the Main Street ramp — usually a one-way passage the other way. As the car leaves the garage, the ramp guard, patrolman Roy E. Vaughn, steps aside to allow the car to pass.

Vaughn: "They were coming backwards, coming up the Main Street ramp....I had to step aside to let the car out. Then I resumed my position a few minutes later — it was very shortly."

11:17 to 11:18 a.m.

Ruby, carrying a .38-caliber Colt Cobra revolver, leaves the nearby Western Union office and walks to the police station basement.

THE EVENTS OF NOV. 24, 1963

According to the Warren Commission report

Lee Harvey Oswald's morning	Jack Ruby's morning
9-10 a.m.	
Police discuss plans to transfer Oswald from city jail to county jail. During the night, Dallas FBI had received anonymous threat that group of 100 to 200 men would attempt to kill Oswald. Basement of Police and Courts Building has been cleared and guards stationed. Oswald is given final interrogation in captain's office.	Ruby, at his apartment in Oak Cliff, reads newspaper item that says Mrs. Kennedy may have to return to Dallas for Oswald's trial. The article and memorial services on television leave him in tears.
10-11 a.m.	
Questioning of Oswald continues. Crowd of reporters and photographers gathers at police station.	Ruby gets a phone call from a stripper at his club. She asks him to send money to her in Fort Worth.
11-11:15 a.m.	
Police change plan for transfer by deciding to move Oswald in police car rather than armored truck.	Ruby drives to Western Union office on Main Street to wire money.
11:17-11:18 a.m.	
Officers escort Oswald to basement.	**1** Ruby, carrying .38-caliber revolver, leaves Western Union office and quickly walks to police station.
	2 A car leaving the garage distracts the officer guarding the ramp. Ruby walks down ramp to basement.

11:21 a.m.

3 Two officers bring Oswald from jail into basement. Another officer backs up car to load Oswald and almost hits Ruby as he jumps out of crowd and fires one shot into Oswald.

11:22 a.m.

4 While police subdue Ruby, officers carry Oswald back into jail office. Oswald is mortally wounded. He is taken to Parkland Memorial Hospital where he is pronounced dead at 1:07 p.m.

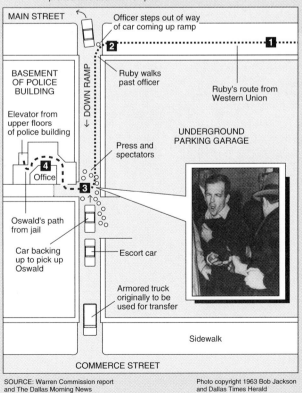

MAIN STREET

Officer steps out of way of car coming up ramp

2 .... **1**

BASEMENT OF POLICE BUILDING

DOWN RAMP →

Ruby walks past officer

Ruby's route from Western Union

Elevator from upper floors of police building

UNDERGROUND PARKING GARAGE

Press and spectators

4 Office

3

Oswald's path from jail

Car backing up to pick up Oswald

Escort car

Armored truck originally to be used for transfer

Sidewalk

COMMERCE STREET

SOURCE: Warren Commission report and The Dallas Morning News

Photo copyright 1963 Bob Jackson and Dallas Times Herald

Officers take Oswald on the elevator to the Police Department basement.

Oswald passes reporters and onlookers on his way to the transfer car.

Ruby: "(I) walked the distance from the Western Union to the (Main Street) ramp — I didn't sneak in. I didn't linger in there. I didn't crouch or hide behind anyone....There was an officer talking...to a Sam Pierce in a car parked up on the curb."

Graves: "It seemed like every darn thing went wrong. Some lieutenant and some patrolman, I guess, two of them in a car wanted to go out (of the basement), and they had that darn big old (armored) truck up there blocking the exit. So they went out the wrong way, and as they went out the wrong way onto Main Street, why, that gave Ruby a chance to just walk in....

"Nobody saw Ruby come in. So he just strolled on down there."

Vaughn: "Sometime later in the morning I learned that allegedly Ruby had told them he came down that (Main Street) ramp....I'll tell you right up front I don't believe it....I think he came in another way."

Radio reporter Pappas: "I tried to squeeze in (to the crowd). What I didn't realize was that I had moved in and pushed in right in front of Jack Ruby."

11:21 a.m.

Dhority is moving Fritz's car to pick up Oswald. The plan is to have Leavelle and Graves ride with Oswald in the back seat, and Fritz and Dhority in the front. Leavelle and Graves, at either side of Oswald, enter the basement. The scene is being broadcast live on national television.

Graves: "When we came out of the jail office door...the car was supposed to be centered in there so all we would have to do was...take several steps to the car in more or less a straight shot.

"But in the confusion...the car was still up a car length, maybe two lengths, from where it was supposed to be...which meant that we had to walk out and turn slightly to the right...which is what we started to do when Ruby jumped in there."

Right: Oswald grimaces as Jack Ruby (right) shoots him in the Police Department basement. The shooting, televised nationally, is witnessed by millions.

Officers struggle with nightclub owner Jack Ruby after the shooting. Ruby is not visible.

Officer L.C. Graves holds the gun used to shoot Oswald.

Dhority: "I went down and got the car and was backing it in to load him....I backed it all the way from the parking spot right up in front of the door where he (Oswald) was coming out....

"I was turned looking around toward Oswald....I saw Ruby run behind it (the car)....I nearly hit him....I just hit the brakes and about that time he whipped out the gun."

Ruby: "I walked down those few steps, and there was the person that — I wouldn't say I saw red — it was a feeling I had for our beloved President and Mrs. Kennedy that he was insignificant to what my purpose was.

"I had the gun in my right pocket and impulsively...I saw him, and that is all I can say. And I didn't care what happened to me.

"I think I used the words 'you killed the president, you rat.' The next thing, I was down on the floor."

Pappas: "Ruby jumped out in front of me and streaked by us and put one bullet in him....It stunned me. It stunned us all....Oswald moaned and he fell."

Bob Jackson, a staff photographer of the Dallas Times Herald, *captures the shooting in a picture that later won a Pulitzer Prize and became the most famous photo from the scene.*

Jackson: "I was already pre-focused on about 11 feet, which helped, and I was pretty ready like everybody was — and then he came out. And I was aware of somebody stepping in front of me off to my right....

"My first thought was, somebody is getting in my way. I didn't think somebody is stepping out to shoot him. Of course, the gun went off and then I knew.... He was shot right on the spot I was focused on."

Graves, Dhority and Don Ray Archer, an auto theft detective, are among those struggling to subdue Ruby.

Graves: "By the time I could get my right arm loose from Oswald and reach over and grab that gun, he had already stepped down and fired one shot right in my face....

"I didn't hear a word from him (Ruby). All Oswald said was (to) let out a big grunt — uhhhh — something to that effect — and began to crumble....

"If he had gotten that gun out of my hand after I got it and wrenched it around where I couldn't take it away from him, he might have...continued shooting it because he was milking on that trigger.

"But having the cylinder anchored in my hand kept it from turning in that .38. You can hold that cylinder and they won't shoot you because the cylinder won't rotate....

"I was telling him, 'Turn it loose! Turn it loose! Turn it loose!' with a few other choice words. And you know what? The officers jumped on him and they durn near pulled him loose from me before I got the gun out of his hand."

Archer: "While we had him down on the basement, I asked, 'Who is it? Who in the heck is it?'...Jack turned around and said, 'I'm Jack Ruby. Y'all know me.'"

Dhority: "When he said that, I just thought to myself, 'You son of a gun, you thought you was going to be a hero.'"

Police guard the Parkland emergency room where Oswald is taken.

11:22 to 11:23 a.m.

Leavelle and detective Billy Combest carry Oswald back inside the jail office.

Leavelle: "I took my keys out of my pocket and had Combest take off the handcuffs."

Dr. Fred Bieberdorf, a medical student and city jail medical attendant who was in the basement, comes to the scene after hearing the shot.

Bieberdorf: "Oswald was lying on the ground without anybody bending over or around him. I bent over there and I saw the bullet wound on his side, and I could actually feel the bullet on the other side. It didn't quite come out, but you could tell…it hit his heart or lungs or liver or spleen.…

"I felt for a pulse, felt for a heartbeat, didn't find any, so I gave him some external cardiac massage with my hand there on the hard surface."

11:24 a.m.

An ambulance arrives at the jail.

Graves: "The ambulance was there and they throwed him on a gurney and shoved him in that ambulance. I got in the jumpseat up close to the front. We had a doctor on duty, an intern (Bieberdorf) from Parkland, (who) stays there all the time. He jumps in there and jumped up on my knees, set up on my lap and pumped his (Oswald's) heart all the way.

"Right after we crossed that railroad track going out to Parkland, he died permanently, as far as I'm concerned, because he gave that dying quiver. He stretched out real stiff and give another one of those moans and then went totally limp."

Bieberdorf: "The ambulance arrived and…they had a hard time. That was back in the days of the primitive ambulances, and they had an oxygen bottle there but they couldn't even find the key to open it.…They didn't even have a stethoscope in the ambulance.… They didn't have any IV bottles.

"I never could find a pulse. He (Oswald) just made a few agonal groans, and I never heard anything out of him.…He wasn't bleeding externally. He just had a bullet hole, I guess it was on his left side…in his chest."

Dhority also rides in the ambulance.

Dhority: "Captain Fritz told me to ride out in the ambulance with Oswald to Parkland hospital and set up security because (Gov. John) Connally was out there. And also to try and get a dying declaration off of Oswald.…

"He looked up at me one time and kind of gurgled with his eyes open but that was all that come out of him."

About 11:25 a.m.

Archer and other officers manage to get Ruby under control.

Archer: "We went upstairs to book him and to guard him to keep him from committing suicide or anything like that until he could be interrogated.

"He really didn't talk going up in the elevator. (Capt.) Glen King said, 'Jack, why in the hell did you do something like this?' And Jack replied at that time (that) he just couldn't stand Jackie (Kennedy) having to come back here (to testify), or something to that extent.

"We were booking him in and…somebody mentioned, 'It's not looking good (for Oswald), Jack.' And he said, 'I intended to shoot him three times, but you guys just moved too fast for me.'

"(Ruby was) very hyper, very nervous. He was perspiring, his chest breathing hard.…He didn't want to talk about why he did this."

11:30 a.m.

Assistant District Attorney Bill Alexander sees Ruby in the city jail.

Alexander: "He didn't feel like that he had done anything wrong.… I used just a little bit of profanity but I asked him what the deal was, and he said, 'You guys couldn't do it.' He felt like he had done a great thing."

11:32 a.m.

Oswald is wheeled into Parkland. Doctors waiting for him include Ronald C. Jones, the hospital's senior surgical resident.

Jones: "He (Oswald) was unconscious when he came in, was unresponsive, did not have a palpable pulse but did have a heartbeat. We did a cut-down, put in an IV in his arm and put a chest tube in his left chest.

"From the time he hit the emergency room until he was in the operating room — because we were ready to go — was only about seven or eight minutes. We took him straight up to the operating room."

11:34 a.m.

In Washington, Jacqueline and Robert Kennedy enter the East Room and the coffin is opened. Mrs. Kennedy places in

UPI/Bettmann Newsphotos

A crowd waits outside the White House gate for the caisson that will carry President Kennedy's coffin to the Capitol.

the coffin three letters — one from her, one from Caroline and a scribbled sheet from John-John — as well as two gifts from her that Kennedy had treasured: a pair of gold cufflinks and a scrimshaw bearing the presidential seal. Robert Kennedy puts in his PT-109 tie pin and an engraved silver rosary.

About 11:40 a.m.

Fry is still giving his sermon at First Presbyterian when he is handed a note saying that an incident has occurred at the City Hall a block away and that the church is surrounded by police.

Fry: "We went on through the service, and then I told the people that there had been a problem up at the City Hall and I didn't know what the nature of it was but that the police had asked that they go out single file, which they did....We had to let the people out one aisle at a time for them to go through the police guard."

Holmes is handed a note near the end of his service at Northaven United Methodist.

Holmes: "The note read that Oswald has just been assassinated. I announced that, and there was a gasp."

11:44 a.m.

Dr. Tom Shires, chief of surgery, hears about the Oswald shooting on his car radio and goes to Parkland. He and Jones are among those who operate on Oswald.

Jones: "It was a fairly straightforward procedure, just opening the abdomen and identifying the injuries and controlling the bleeding, and as soon as we did that he lost blood pressure again and his heart stopped from hemorrhage....

"I'm not sure that with all the injuries that he had if he'd been shot in the operating room that we would have salvaged him. It blew a major blood vessel off the front of his aorta, which is the largest artery in the body...and the inferior vena cava was injured, and the renal artery and vein was injured and the right kidney....

"He never really developed normal blood pressure from the time we started until we stopped. He did get minimal blood pressure but never regained consciousness....

"I think you knew that you were dealing with somebody that was going to be known in history and was known already around the world. And so you knew that if you could you would save him."

12:08 p.m.

Kennedy's coffin begins its journey from the White House to the Capitol. President and Mrs. Johnson ride in a limousine with the Kennedy family.

Mrs. Johnson: "As soon as we emerged from the gates of the White House, I became aware of that sea of faces stretching away on every side — silent, watching faces.

"I wanted to cry for them and with them, but it was impossible to permit the catharsis of tears. I don't know quite why, except that perhaps continuity of strength demands restraint. Another reason was that the dignity of Mrs. Kennedy and the members of the family demanded it....

"The feeling persisted that I was moving, step by step, through a Greek tragedy."

Funeral home manager Hagan: "The president's body was borne on a horse-drawn caisson. That was at full procession, with the police marching unit, the commanding general, muffled drums — no other instruments were used — the detail of Navy enlisted men as honorary pallbearers, special honor guard, national color detail. It was spectacular."

Accompanying the caisson is Pfc. Arthur A. Carlson, whose job in the Army's 3rd Infantry Old Guard is to lead a riderless horse in the funerals of high-ranking officials. He leads the spirited Black Jack, carrying a saddle with riding boots turned backward in the stirrups — symbolic of a fallen leader.

UPI/Bettmann Newsphotos

Jacqueline Kennedy, John-John and Caroline wait outside the White House before Kennedy's coffin is carried to the Capitol.

Mrs. Johnson: "The only time the attorney general said anything else was when we passed a big building on the left, and he looked over and said...'That was where it all began. That was where he ran for the presidency.'

"His face was grave, white, sorrowful, and there was a flinching of the jaw at that moment that almost made — well, it made your soul flinch for him."

12:47 p.m.

The procession reaches Capitol Hill.

12:52 p.m.

Outside the Capitol Rotunda, a 21-gun salute is fired. The body bearers, who include Marine Lance Cpl. Tim Cheek, carry the coffin up the steep steps; at the top, they stop and hold it while the Navy Band plays Hail to the Chief. *Lt. Bird and a sergeant move in and seize the handles on the ends to help the bearers support the tremendous weight.*

Cheek: "The sergeant in front, I could see his body quivering with the weight."

The coffin is moved inside the building, where government officials, Kennedy friends and family members have gathered for a short ceremony.

Honor guard member Perrault: "There was quite an audience....I recall former presidents, speakers of the house, practically every member of Congress.... Just seeing every walk of life and costumes of the different nationalities and so forth coming through there."

Carlson: "He had tiny little feet so they didn't ride him, nobody rode him, but he was a fairly good-looking horse, and so they used him for that job almost exclusively. I guess that was his job and mine."

At Parkland, Landregan releases a statement to reporters.

Landregan: "Dr. Tom Shires, chief of surgery at Parkland Memorial Hospital and Southwestern Medical School, advises me that Lee Oswald is currently undergoing surgery for a single gunshot wound that entered on his left side and did not exit. The patient is in extremely critical condition."

About 12:30 p.m.

In the Kennedy-Johnson limousine, Robert Kennedy admonishes John-John, who is jumping from the back seat to the front, to be good, and promises him a flag.

About 1 p.m.

In Dallas, police Capt. Fritz asks detective Rose to search Ruby's Oak Cliff apartment.

Rose: "I really didn't find anything of significance there. I brought in some documents....I was looking for any

Honor guards accompany the caisson bearing Kennedy's coffin.

The caisson leaves the White House for the Capitol.

writings maybe that would implicate him (Ruby) in the assassination. I never did find it."

Parkland issues a second news bulletin.

Landregan: "Lee Oswald has suffered a massive injury of abdomen with injuries to the major vessels. Bleeding has been controlled. A cardiac arrest has developed. The patient's left chest has been opened and cardiac massage begun."

Some minutes later, Robert Oswald arrives at Parkland.

Assistant administrator Pete Geilich: "Oswald's brother was brought in and placed in the volunteers' office. He was asked if he wanted to talk to the press. He was sobbing, 'No, no. Not at this time.'"

1:02 p.m.

In the Rotunda, Senate Majority Leader Mike Mansfield begins to speak.

Mansfield: "There was a sound of laughter; in a moment, it was no more. And so she took a ring from her finger and placed it in his hands...."

"There was a man marked with the scars of his love of country, a body active with the surge of a life far, far from spent and, in a moment, it was no more. And so she took a ring from her finger and placed it in his hands.

"There was a husband who asked much and gave much, and out of the giving and the asking, wove with a woman what could not be broken in life, and in a moment it was no more. And so she took a ring from her finger and placed it in his hands, and kissed him and closed the lid of a coffin."

1:07 p.m.

Oswald is pronounced dead.

1:17 p.m.

After Kennedy is eulogized by Mansfield, Chief Justice Earl Warren and House Speaker John McCormack, Mrs. Kennedy and her daughter kneel by the coffin and kiss the flag.

Body bearer Felder: "Mrs. Kennedy and Caroline went over to the coffin and put a hand on it. In fact she (Caroline) put her hand under the flag to touch it. It was a very emotional moment for all of us."

1:19 p.m.

The Kennedy party leaves Capitol Hill.

1:25 p.m.

Chief of surgery Shires announces Oswald's death. Oswald's body is taken to the morgue at Parkland.

Assistant administrator Landregan: "I was the hospital's representative at the autopsy....I remember a law enforcement officer at the end of the table with a shotgun, standing there the whole time. I don't know what they expected — that Oswald was going to get up and

Behind the caisson are Pfc. Arthur A. Carlson and Black Jack, carrying a saddle with riding boots turned backward, symbolizing a fallen leader.

Black Star: Flip Schulke

try to escape or that somebody was going to break in and do something to the body or what."

1:28 p.m.

The Kennedy party returns to the White House. The Rotunda, meanwhile, is opened to the public, and hundreds of thousands gather throughout the afternoon and evening to view the coffin.

Funeral home manager Hagan: "As far as you wanted to look there were people. Most of them were crying. The tragic death, the assassination of a young president who had enjoyed immense popularity — and all of a sudden, it's all over. And we were not ready for that. A state of shock existed everywhere."

About 1:30 p.m.

Marina and Marguerite Oswald drive to the Paine residence in Irving to pick up some fresh clothes and diapers.

Marguerite Oswald: "We got to Irving. There is police cars all around....As soon as the car stopped, the Secret Service agent said, 'Lee has been shot.' And I said 'How badly?' He said, 'In the shoulder.'

"I cried and I said, 'Marina, Lee has been shot.'...

"I am sitting in the car with the (Secret Service) agent (Mike Howard). Marina is in the home now. So something comes over the mike, and the Secret Service agent says, 'Do not repeat. Do not repeat.'

"I said, 'My son is gone, isn't he?' And he didn't answer. I said, 'Answer me. I want to know. If my son is gone, I want to meditate.' He said, 'Yes, Mrs. Oswald, your son has just expired.'

"When I got the news, I went into the home, and I said, 'Marina, our boy is gone.'"

1 to 2 p.m.

Word of Oswald's death reaches the Dallas Police Department. Archer is with Secret Service agent Sorrels and Sgt. Pat Dean.

Archer: "I said, well, Ruby hasn't really given us any reason or anything up to this point. I said he's talking about his childhood in Chicago, he's talking about the clubs he's owned here in Dallas, he's talked about the old Silver Spur he used to own on Ervay Street."

Sorrels suggests that Archer tell Ruby about Oswald's death.

Archer: "I said, 'Jack, it looks like it might be the electric chair for you. They just told me that Oswald's dead.'...

"I had really expected him to become more tense....He had been borrowing cigarettes from me. He had been smoking some cigarettes....But when I told him he was dead, his demeanor completely

An American flag on the U.S. Capitol waves above the caisson carrying President Kennedy's body.

The horse-drawn caisson reaches the steps of the Capitol.

changed. He was more relaxed, he quit perspiring, his hard breathing had stopped.

"And I said, 'Do you understand that you might go to the electric chair?' He said, 'Well, is Captain Fritz going to come up and talk to me?' and I said, 'I'm sure they'll be sending somebody.'

"He said, 'Well, I would like to go down as soon as I could. Do you think they'll give me an opportunity to call my attorney?' I said, 'I'm sure they will.'

"Then I said, 'Would you like a cigarette?' And he said, 'Oh, no, no. I don't smoke.'"

About 1:45 p.m.

Mrs. Kennedy, who had seen an eternal flame in France, asks for one to be prepared for her husband. Her friends and advisers are hesitant, worried it might be seen as ostentatious, but the Pentagon is asked to fashion a flame. The request is handed to Lt. Col. Bernard Carroll, Fort Myer's post engineer.

Carroll: "Most shops that furnish gas and copper tubing and whatever we needed were closed. So my assistant and I sat down over in the cemetery office with two sets of Yellow Pages. My assistant took the one for Virginia, and I took the one for Maryland.

"We went down the list of supply houses…and after probably an hour I called a place in Maryland and a man answered the phone. I told him what I wanted, and he said, 'I'll be glad to get you anything you want.' And they brought down all the supplies.…

"There was no panic. There was a sense of having a job to do and having to get things done and having to do them in a hurry."

About 2 p.m.

Marguerite and Marina Oswald are driven by Secret Service agents to Parkland.

Associated Press

Rays of sunlight bathe the coffin during a short ceremony in the Capitol Rotunda attended by government officials, friends and family members.

Marguerite Oswald: "They didn't want us to see Lee, the ugliness of it, evidently. But I insisted, and so did Marina.

"On the way in the car they are trying to get us to change our minds. Mike Howard said, 'I want you to know when we get there we will not be able to protect you. Our security measures end right there. The police will then have you under protection.'…

"I said, 'That is fine. If I am to die, I will die that way. But I am going to see my son.'"

Assistant administrator Geilich sees the two women when they arrive.

Geilich: "The mother was quite upset, but the wife merely had a look of shock about her. The look on her face was not unlike that on Mrs. Kennedy's face two days earlier."

The two women see Oswald's body.

UPI/Bettmann Newsphotos

Mourners gather at the Rotunda during the eulogy by Senate Majority Leader Mike Mansfield.

Marguerite Oswald: "Lee's body was on a hospital bed, I would say, or a table.…Marina went first. She opened his eyelids. I am a nurse, and I don't think I could have done that. This is a very, very strong girl, that she can open a dead man's eyelids. And she says, 'He cry. He eye wet.' To the doctor. And the doctor said, 'Yes.'

"While leaving the room, I said to the police, 'I think some day you will hang your heads in shame.'"

Jacqueline Kennedy kisses the flag on her husband's coffin. Also kneeling is their daughter, Caroline, who slips her hand beneath the flag.

Marina Oswald and daughter, June, arrive at Parkland Memorial Hospital.

2:06 p.m.

Dallas police officials ask Dr. Bieberdorf to talk to Ruby.

Bieberdorf: "They were concerned that Ruby might commit suicide, so they sent me in to talk to him....

"Ruby said, 'I know they're worried about me committing suicide, killing myself. I'm not going to and do what you need to.' I said, 'They want to do a (strip search)'...and he said, 'That's fine.'...

"They'd lost one prisoner; they didn't want to lose another....They were concerned with why would somebody do this unless they were going to kill themselves right afterward.

"He didn't seem upset, just being perfectly normal, like you'd meet him on the street. He was not incoherent....He wasn't bragging or proud of himself either."

3:15 p.m.

Ruby is brought to Fritz's office for questioning and arraignment on a charge of murdering Oswald.

Late Sunday afternoon

In Washington, the crowds outside the Capitol Rotunda continue to swell. Joan Pounds, a Washington housekeeper, has been standing in line for hours.

Ms. Pounds: "We left home at 6 on Sunday morning and we never did get to the Rotunda....The line was long, and it moved very slow. We finally left at 6 that night....It was just that we wanted to pay our respects. It affected everybody all over the world, not just us, and we wanted to pay our respects. He was my favorite president."

Jim Clark, a 20-year-old student at the University of Texas at Austin, has traveled to Washington and has been standing in line for several hours to see the coffin.

Clark: "It was a feeling that this was something I needed to do."

Inside, the honor guard stands watches of 30 minutes on, two hours off.

Perrault: "Whenever we were off watch, we were in the old Senate chamber....We had a little freedom to step back into the Rotunda out of the limelight and just observe. At one time, I stepped outside to look out over the Capitol steps, and listening to the radio, for 22 city blocks people were waiting in line....

"I hadn't ever seen anything like that. People were lined up outside the Rotunda as far as you could see. How could one single thing bring all those people together like that?"

At the White House, officials discuss the funeral procession to be held Monday to St. Matthew's.

Busby: "Somehow the word got out that the new president would walk in the procession....People started calling me from all around the country — 'Stop this madness, he mustn't be out on the streets.'

"Regular people, corporate executives, nearly all of whom I didn't know. People

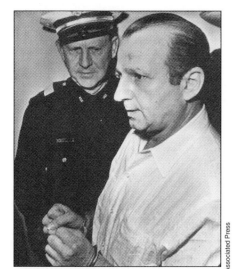

Jack Ruby walks through the city jail to be arraigned on murder charges.

were indignant and angry. I finally called the head of the Secret Service and told him this was the reaction that was developing, people were scared to death.

"But Johnson felt strongly that you mustn't let people like assassins take control of the streets."

Some officials are thinking even further ahead. Deputy U.S. Attorney General Nicholas Katzenbach ponders the investigation that will have to be held.

Katzenbach: "I began thinking about what ended up as the Warren Commission…what you had in the past, and I was primarily thinking of Lincoln, all that speculation through the years about who really was behind it and what really happened.…I wrote a memo…Monday (suggesting that Johnson appoint a federal commission)."

Mrs. Johnson reflects on the emotionally draining events of the day.

Mrs. Johnson: "To me, one of the saddest things in the whole tragedy was that Mrs. Kennedy achieved on this desperate day something she had never quite achieved in the years she'd been in the White House — a state of love, a state of rapport between herself and the people of this country.

Jacqueline Kennedy, holding the hands of Caroline and John-John, descends the steps of the Capitol. Kennedy family members and the Johnsons follow.

"Her behavior from the moment of the shot until I last saw her was, to me, one of the most memorable things of all."

In Dallas, officials are beginning to work on the details of a burial service for Oswald. The Rev. Carl A. Gaertner, pastor

of Zion Lutheran Church, is contacted, though he is not ultimately the one who performs the service.

Gaertner: "One of the government agencies called late Sunday afternoon and asked whether I'd be willing to

have the committal (burial) service for Oswald. I said I'd be willing to do it only if I could talk with the family....He (the Secret Service agent) gave me the telephone number of the motel where the family was staying."

Dallas Morning News nightclub columnist Tony Zoppi tries to see Ruby at the jail.

Zoppi: "All of the press was there, and (because Oswald had been killed) they were insulting the cops something awful. They were calling the cops every name in the book....And the cops were under strict orders not to make waves, so they kind of gritted their teeth. It was just awful."

Carie Welch, Dallas mayor pro tem, and other City Council members are leaving a memorial Mass for Kennedy at Sacred Heart Cathedral when they are approached for comments about Dallas by a reporter for CBS News.

Welch: "We were all doing our best to reflect that Dallas was a positive, wholesome community, one not given to this type of violence, that it was unfortunate that it (Kennedy's assassination) happened, but it could have happened anywhere in the world....

"We were not ever going to reflect that this was the attitude of the people of Dallas at that time....Dallas was known as a hospitable city and not a hostile city. Dallas had a very polished, untarnished image at that time, and we were right in the midst of a very healthy growth pattern....

"We were all totally sympathetic and appalled that this had happened in our city."

About 6 p.m.

Eva Grant goes to the jail to visit her brother, Jack Ruby.

Mrs. Grant: "My brother didn't tell me anything. He was crying....Someone said, 'Did you ask him why he did it?' I

says, 'No.' Because I tell you the truth, my brother looked a little crazy....

"I was crying. I was carrying on. He says, 'Don't worry about me.'...I says, 'I'm glad Ma and Pa is dead. They don't see you in jail, they don't know about you being in jail.'...

"He didn't say nothing. He didn't answer."

A Secret Service agent contacts Paul J. Groody, director of Miller's Funeral Home in Fort Worth, about arrangements for Oswald's funeral.

Groody: "I remember that I was scared. We didn't know who this guy (Oswald) really was. You have to think in terms of what life was like back then, and we really did think this was the beginning of World War III.

"I was called about 6 o'clock (Sunday evening) and we went to Parkland, but it was at least 11 p.m. before we were able to get the body released....

"They (authorities) roped off the entire triangle around where the funeral home was located....

"The Secret Service wanted me to do it as secretly as I could and not put out any information. We were scared because the president had already been shot and now Oswald was shot. I didn't know if some other nut was going to shoot the dumb undertaker."

After 7:30 p.m.

Rev. Gaertner calls Oswald's brother.

Gaertner: "I told him I was a Lutheran minister and had been asked if I would officiate at a committal service, and he responded: 'We don't want just a committal service. We want a big funeral; with a church in Fort Worth.'

"I told him that the Secret Service wanted to keep it very quiet, and he insisted it had to be one of the larger churches in Fort Worth.

"I said that under the circumstances, with emotions in the community and nation running so high, that I didn't think it would be a good idea."

Sunday evening

In Washington, dozens of foreign dignitaries and heads of state are arriving for the Kennedy funeral. Undersecretary of State George Ball greets them.

Ball: "We went out to Dulles (airport), and (Secretary of State Dean) Rusk and I took turns all night long greeting these heads of state and foreign dignitaries. There were a vast number.

"It was a pretty impressive lot of characters....(Charles) de Gaulle was very eloquent. He said, 'I haven't come on my own, I've been sent by the people of France.'"

A small group of the Johnsons' friends gathers at The Elms for dinner. Those present include John Connally III, 17.

Connally: "Everyone was very saddened. The president and Mrs. Johnson were very upset. He was trying to consult with people about how to get going, how to keep going with the government. The grief was such that everyone was talking in hushed tones....

"After dinner people were sitting around in groups of twos and threes. Sometime that evening we went to the Rotunda and paid our respects to President Kennedy, who was lying in state. We went in through a back way."

8:04 p.m.

Mrs. Kennedy and Robert Kennedy revisit the Rotunda. Allen J. Eldredge, a sergeant first class in the Army, is on duty in the Rotunda.

Eldredge: "No one was around the coffin because it was kind of personal. I was standing near the main entrance of the

---

Left: After the Capitol Rotunda is opened to the public, hundreds of thousands of people file past to view the flag-draped coffin of President John F. Kennedy.

Rotunda. She went up and put her hand on the coffin. Then I think she knelt down. I had to turn away — a lot of people did. I doubt if there was a dry eye in that Rotunda. It was so sad."

Late Sunday evening

Concerned about the weight of the coffin and the steep steps that the body bearers will have to descend from the Capitol on Monday, Lt. Bird has his team practice on the steps at Arlington cemetery's Tomb of the Unknowns with a standard military coffin weighted with sandbags.

Felder: "We had to wait until everyone was gone, because you didn't want people seeing you out there rehearsing with a coffin....

"We've got a couple of them at the fort we used for rehearsals and training. In this particular incidence, we went further to get the feel for the weight. We had two guys (Lt. Bird and the tomb guard) sit on top of it as we went up and down the steps."

French President Charles de Gaulle (left) is met by Secretary of State Dean Rusk on his arrival at Washington's Dulles International Airport.

About 11 p.m.

At Arlington cemetery, the grave has been dug with a backhoe and the temporary holder for the eternal flame constructed. Fort Myer engineer Carroll makes last-minute checks on the flame.

Carroll: "We did a final check at midnight....When we got ready to light the flame somebody had to be with the switch over in a hiding place, and at a signal that man would turn on a valve and a match would be held to the flame and it would ignite.

"The plan was that we would have tapers for Mrs. Kennedy to light it. They were made of a piece of welding rod crimped at one end with a piece of gun cloth.

"And everything was all set. It worked."

Near midnight

About 75,600 people have filed past Kennedy's coffin. Officials had planned to close the Rotunda at 8 p.m. but then decided to keep it open as long as people wanted to come. Realizing the size of the crowd, they start having people go by two abreast in each of two lines past the cof-

fin. Now people are filing by at the rate of 14,400 an hour.

Sen. Yarborough and his wife, from their apartment looking toward the Capitol, watch the crowds gather all night long.

Yarborough: "The crowds...were lined up for blocks....We stood up that night and watched them and talked about the future....We could hear footsteps on the cobblestone, on the sidewalk....

"(It was) very quiet. I never heard a voice spoken. People were dealing with their own thoughts about what had happened to their world, as we were."

NOV. 25
MONDAY

1:03 a.m.

The line on Capitol Hill is three miles long.

6 a.m.

Dr. Louis A. Saunders, executive secretary with the Fort Worth Area Council of Churches, hears on the radio that Oswald's body is being taken to Fort Worth for burial.

Saunders: "Before I left home, I called this Mr. Groody, the undertaker, and told him I just wanted to be sure that a minister was available to perform the funeral service. I was assured that arrangements for that were being made."

Reporters, including Mike Cochran of The Associated Press, begin to gather soon after dawn at Rose Hill Cemetery, which Marguerite Oswald has selected as the burial site.

Cochran: "We really had no idea when it (the burial) was going to take place. I think I got there after sunup....They not only had nobody to carry the coffin, but they had to recruit someone to perform the service."

8:05 a.m.

The last visitors go by Kennedy's coffin in the Rotunda. About 250,000 people have filed past the coffin.

9 a.m.

Confusion develops over who will hold the Oswald services as the Secret Service contacts Gaertner, pastor of the Zion

Jacqueline Kennedy kneels at the foot of the coffin when she returns to the Capitol Rotunda on Monday.

Associated Press

Lutheran Church, and Fry, of First Pres-byterian Church.

Gaertner: "I told the Secret Service that I was willing to do it....They said they would call me back."

Fry: "They asked me if I could bury Lee Harvey Oswald, and I swallowed hard and said yes....I've never refused to bury anybody. You may not want to do it, but you do it....

"(Later) they called me back and said it (the arrangements) had been done over in Fort Worth."

Saunders, meanwhile, goes to Farrington Field to make arrangements for a memorial service for Kennedy. On his way back to the office, he listens to preparations for the Kennedy funeral on the radio.

Saunders: "I remembered Oswald....I was afraid that with everything that was going on, this was just going to fall through the cracks, and I didn't want people to think that if no minister was there, that was a reflection on the Christian community in Fort Worth....

"I didn't want to do the service myself because I was not an active pastor at the time. I just wanted to make sure there was one available. When I got to my office I called the funeral home again and the Secret Service in Dallas and was assured everything was taken care of."

About 9:40 a.m.

Jacqueline, Robert and Ted Kennedy kneel by the coffin in the Rotunda and pray.

9:45 a.m.

The body bearers, wearing white cotton gloves that have been dampened to improve their grip, carry the coffin out of the Rotunda.

Body bearer Felder: "This was the part we were all frightened of. We wet our gloves and prepared, took a good grip and Lieutenant Bird was right behind. We got it down the steps no problem, breathed a sigh of relief, and put it onto the caisson."

About 9:50 a.m.

The procession leaves Capitol Hill for the White House and then St. Matthew's. Larry O'Brien is in the White House.

UPI/Bettmann Newsphotos

A military team carries the coffin down the steep Capitol steps.

O'Brien: "We were observing the ceremonial aspects of all this in the Capitol and the departure from the Capitol (on television). And the little boy we knew at that time called John-John was in the room looking at the screen. He came into the room where Dave Powers and I were and saluted the screen.

"One of the White House ushers, we said to him, 'Get us a bottle of champagne,' which he did, and we poured glasses, the three of us, Powers, O'Donnell and I. While still watching the unfolding on the screen, we raised our glasses and said, 'To the president.'

"Then we left the White House and joined the procession as it passed the White House."

10 to 11 a.m.

Many Dallas-area churches hold memorial services; some set up televisions so that parishioners can also watch the national services. A large interdenominational service at Fort Worth's Farrington Field draws about 5,000 people. The speakers include the Rev. Granville Walker, pastor of University Christian Church in Fort Worth.

Walker: "I guess the most spectacular thing about the service was that it was one of the very few times when Catholics, Jews and Protestants got together. That is something we do a lot more often now, but that wasn't the case back in 1963."

10:30 a.m.

Chief of protocol Duke arranges the procession on foot from the White House to St. Matthew's.

Duke: "I asked the chiefs of state to step forward, and to my intense, amazed relief they all fit in one line across the north driveway. There were 11 of them. The prime ministers were all behind them, but it didn't matter about the prime ministers.

"I wanted each of those chiefs of state not to have to march behind anybody

Crowds line the streets to watch the caisson as it moves through the capital.

Leaders from West Germany, France, Greece, Belgium, Ethiopia and the Philippines walk in the funeral procession.

else. I didn't want to have the president of Germany pushed behind the president of France, for example. I wanted them all to march in equal rank, and, by God, they did."

Officials are worried about security as so many U.S. and foreign dignitaries walk to the Mass. Undersecretary of State Ball forgoes the ceremonies and waits in the

communications center at the State Department in case an emergency arises.

Ball: "I had a feeling that somebody in some authority had to stay in the department because of the possibilities of another assassination taking place as this procession walked through a crowded section of Washington.

"It was madness, it seems to me, but it was Jacqueline Kennedy's idea and we

Attorney General Robert Kennedy, Jacqueline Kennedy and Sen. Edward Kennedy walk near St. Matthew's Cathedral.

couldn't talk Jackie out of it. She wanted that....There was no incident, fortunately, but we were scared to death there was going to be."

10:35 a.m.

The caisson arrives at the White House; Mrs. Kennedy takes her place behind it, with Robert and Ted Kennedy, to walk to the cathedral. John Connally III is among those walking.

Connally: "You have to remember everyone was nervous, highly nervous after the assassination. This was a couple days later, and no one knew if there were going to be other attempts.

"I walked in the funeral procession with the Kennedy family to the cathedral....That's a fairly long walk....I was never conscious of the distance. I never even thought about it....

"We were walking right behind the Kennedy family, and I was right off President Johnson's shoulder."

Johnson: "I remember marching behind the caisson to St. Matthew's Cathedral. The muffled rumble of drums set up a heartbreaking echo."

Just before 11:14 a.m.

Ushers seat the marchers in St. Matthew's.

The funeral procession moves slowly up Connecticut Avenue. Walking behind the caisson are Kennedy family members.

Duke: "We planned the St. Matthew's seating very carefully. We had the heads of state in the first pew, and there was room for five in that first pew. But the emperor of Ethiopia put his sword and his hat on the seat next to him, so that when the president of France came, he occupied the next seat, so that it threw the whole seating off all the way through the whole church.

"Somehow or another the prime minister of Jamaica...didn't have a place to sit. I saw Nelson Rockefeller, then governor of the state of New York, sitting in an aisle seat, so I went over to him, and I said, 'Governor, we have a problem here,

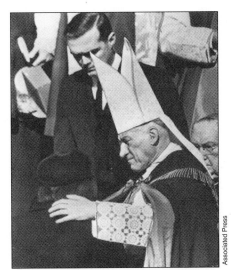

Cardinal Richard Cushing greets Jacqueline Kennedy as she arrives at St. Matthew's Cathedral for the funeral Mass.

could you possibly surrender your seat?' He got up and order was restored."

11:14 a.m.

The coffin enters St. Matthew's and Mass begins.

Duke: "It was just about the best America could produce — meaningful, democratic, sincere, sorrowful, no phony emotion of any kind. It brought out the best in everybody. Everybody was deeply, sincerely moved."

Among those attending the Mass are John Maguire, Ed Drewitch, George "Barney" Ross and Gerald Zinser, all PT-109 crew members whom Kennedy had helped save in August 1943. Zinser is not aware that the other three are present.

Zinser: "Jackie...sent me a pass to get into the church services....There weren't too many (regular) people that got in there, mostly all the high dignitaries like Charles de Gaulle....So it was quite a thing for somebody like me to go to a function like that."

Drewitch: "It was so sad. The eulogy, of course, was very touching....There were multitudes of people, and it seemed

Cardinal Cushing conducts a funeral Mass before President Kennedy's coffin at St. Matthew's Cathedral.

like half were crying....It was a very moving funeral. It was very solemn."

11:15 a.m.

Keith Clark, a bugler in the Army band, reports to Arlington National Cemetery, nearly three hours before he is to play taps at Kennedy's funeral.

Clark: "The military goes crazy on dry runs and being there ahead of time. So I was to be there ready to play at 12:15 (EST); I played at 3:08. It was a rainy day, and we weren't allowed to wear overcoats. So I stood there in the drizzle for three hours. It's normal in the military."

Noon

In Dallas, preparations are made for Ruby's transfer to the county jail.

Capt. Fritz: "We had about the same threats on him that we did with Oswald."

Fritz arranges for Ruby to be taken down the Police Department elevator without fanfare and to be hustled through photographers and reporters into a waiting car.

Fritz: "They shot him right through those people and they didn't even get pictures, and we had him lie down on the back seat and two officers lean back over him, and we drove him...into the jail entrance, didn't even tell the jailer we were coming, and put him in the jail. It worked all right."

Meanwhile, Oswald's body is transported to Rose Hill Cemetery.

Funeral director Groody: "When we arrived at the cemetery, there was a

Associated Press

The Kennedys leave St. Matthew's behind the president's coffin.

Associated Press

Caroline Kennedy looks up at her mother as the family leaves St. Matthew's.

"I don't think anyone ever actually did that, but that's what we were faced with."

12:05 p.m.

At St. Matthew's, Cardinal Richard Cushing of Boston, saying prayers in Latin, suddenly switches to English.

Cushing: "May the angels, dear Jack, lead you into paradise. May the martyrs receive you at your coming."

12:21 p.m.

The coffin has been taken out of the cathedral and put on the gun carriage. The band plays Hail to the Chief, *and Mrs. Kennedy whispers to her small son, who raises his right hand in a salute.*

Powers: "We used to salute around the White House a lot.…Heads of state used to come into the White House and John would be in the balcony, even as a little boy, and he'd see them all saluting. He was always great at saluting, except sometimes he'd salute with his left hand. But that day he was perfect."

12:30 p.m.

The funeral motorcade leaves St. Matthew's. Frederick Case, a clarinet player in the Marine Band, has been waiting outside.

Case: "We stood outside right in our places and froze.…We were allowed to relax but not to go anywhere.…After Mass there…we led the funeral cortege to Arlington cemetery.…

"To see Americans standing 8 to 10 feet deep along a 7-mile funeral route to get a look at a flag-draped caisson go by is one of the most moving sights in my time with the band.…

"He (Kennedy) was such a personable man.…We (the band) just liked him and loved him. Whether you agreed with his politics or not, you almost felt

policeman behind every tombstone just about. Security was very, very tight.…

"We tried to handle it as we would any other burial. It was a matter of respect for fellow man.

"There was one cemetery that had told me they would have space but later called me and told me that he couldn't be buried there because people would object.

"Even the owner of the (Rose Hill) cemetery called me the next morning, saying people were threatening to move out (loved ones) from the cemetery because we buried him there.

Right: John F. Kennedy Jr. salutes his father's coffin outside St. Matthew's Cathedral. The day of the funeral was John-John's third birthday.

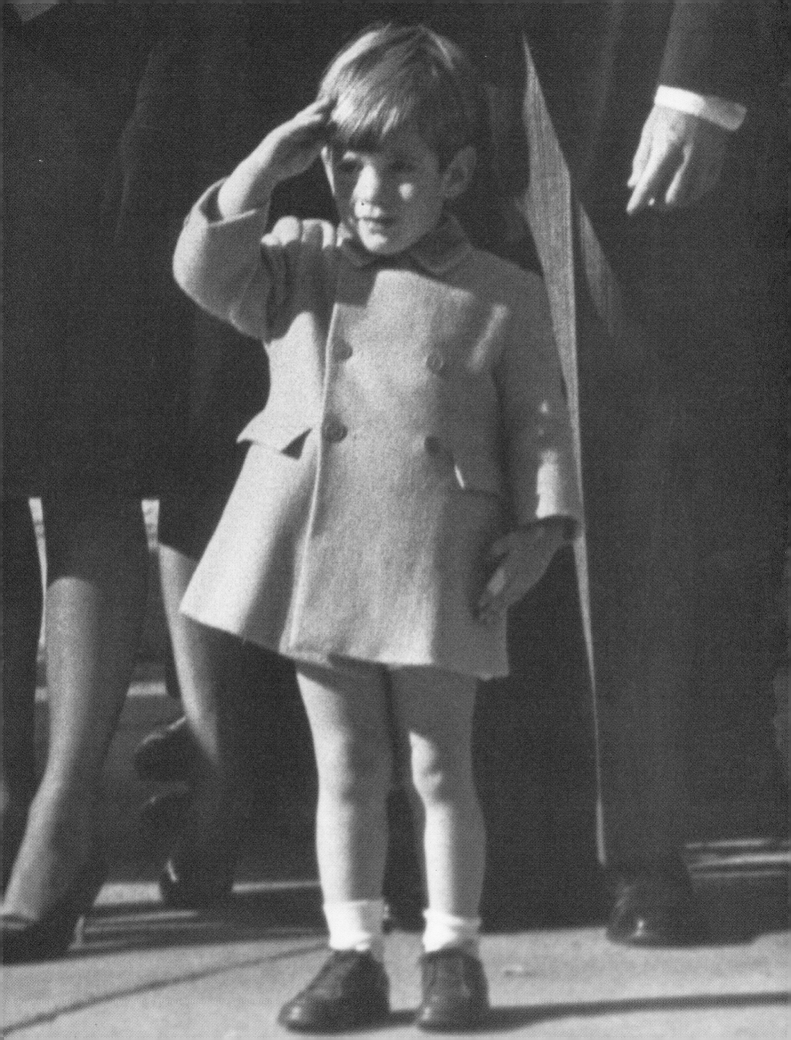

Associated Press

The funeral cortege crosses Memorial Bridge in Washington en route to Arlington National Cemetery. In the background is the Lincoln Memorial.

had a frightened look, like, what are we going to do now?...

"It was the saddest thing you ever saw. Some of them were sadder, they told me later in letters, than if a relative had died."

University of Texas student Clark is standing on a street as the cortege passes.

Clark: "I remember seeing Robert Kennedy ride by in a car...staring blankly out the window....It was just a bare, cold solemn atmosphere...bleak and wintry."

Secret Service agent Youngblood, too, is struck by the mood.

Youngblood: "It was sort of a silence that was so different. I could actually hear people sobbing. It (the funeral procession) was a slow-moving thing. There was nobody trying to run out into the street or alongside. People had tears streaming down their faces."

About 1:30 p.m.

Air Force One is circling between Andrews Air Force Base and Washington, awaiting a signal to begin its run for the Arlington National Cemetery flyby.

Pilot James B. Swindal: "We wanted to get as close as we could, safely, without interfering with Washington National (Airport) traffic so it wouldn't take us too long to get there once we were cleared to do it."

Black Jack, the riderless horse, prances nervously behind the caisson, and Carlson is worried that the horse might bolt from his grip.

Carlson: "There was quite a bit of doubt in my mind whether I would make it....Just the constant strain of handling the horse so many hours and in his state."

with his politics or not, you almost felt like you lost a member of your family....

"It was quite emotional. It still strikes me today that the bandsmen seemed to ...be as personally affected by it.

"There was a feeling that what had happened was an assault on the American system, not just one man or a leader but to our whole system. We're sort of a living symbol of what our country is about."

As the funeral procession leaves the cathedral, PT-109 crew members Maguire, Drewitch and Ross get in Ross' car and fall in at the end of the procession.

Maguire: "Ross had a 10-year-old junk car. We rode at the end of the funeral procession to Arlington....We kinda got in on the tail end. Nobody bothered us. The line must have been a mile long."

12:35 p.m.

Dave Powers stares out from the window of his car in the motorcade, looking at the people lining the streets.

Powers: "You could see it in their faces, all along the way. Some of them

Shortly before 1:54 p.m.

The procession arrives at Arlington cemetery. As U.S. and foreign officials and Kennedy family members gather around the grave site, the Marine Band plays The Star-Spangled Banner, *followed by the Air Force bagpipes with* Mist-Covered Mountain. *The coffin is raised from the caisson and carried to the grave.*

The long walk is taking its toll on the marchers, including sousaphone player Ed Simmons and the team of body bearers.

Simmons: "I thought as we were going up to the grave site, because it was quite a steep hill, that my God, there are muscles I haven't used in months. We were very tired, but you never heard one person complain....

"Probably what sticks in my mind most was the type of coffin, the humongous weight of it and seeing these...body bearers struggling to carry it up the hill to the grave site. It was really a struggle."

Body bearer Felder: "We were tired when we got over there...(and) we still had an eighth of a mile to go up the hill to the site....

"When we took it (the coffin) off the caisson and started marching up the hill to the grave site, the pace was so slow and the priest was walking so slow that we caught up to them and were almost nudging them.

"The guy behind me was saying, 'I'm losing my grip, I'm losing my grip.' I said, 'Let go and grab it again, and I'll hold it up here.' The slow pace, it just felt like we were being pulled into the ground.

"We got to the grave site, and Lieutenant Bird saw the grimace on our faces and stepped up and gave us some relief. At one point I thought we were going to have to set it down on the ground before we got there."

1:54 p.m.

Fifty jet fighters, flying in a V formation with the last plane missing to symbolize

With the Kennedy family nearby, a military team places the president's coffin at the grave site.

the fallen leader, roar over the cemetery, and then Air Force One dips its wings over the grave.

Metzler: "The most difficult thing, I think, of the whole bit — they wanted that flyby to come as the body was approaching the grave.

"Now when you give the signal to go, they're going to be there in 10 minutes. And as it turned out, they flew over just as the body got to the grave."

Swindal: "We were in radio contact with the radar controller at Washington National Airport....We could see the fighter planes also. We knew we'd follow them. They were so much faster, they got a little ahead of us, but we did OK....

"Once the fighters went we were right behind them. We dipped our wings and made a big circle right back to Andrews and landed."

Assistant press secretary Kilduff: "Suddenly, seeing this flight of fighters come across, just screaming jets, with one plane missing from the formation — that was heart-wrenching. Then Air Force One coming across the same way.

"I never saw a plane that size fly so low in my life. And it came over and dipped its wings before it took off and gained altitude."

Powers: "I can remember Air Force One, flying over. He loved that plane."

1:55 to 2:06 p.m.

The Irish cadets execute a silent drill. Cardinal Cushing conducts the commitment. A 21-gun salute and three volleys of rifle fire echo across the cemetery.

Felder: "We are trained not to get emotional about burial details. That was the one time I had to really restrain myself from viewing the family. There were so many, it was difficult not to glance over there out of the corner of your eye.

"I think that's the first time it really hit me as to who I was burying. After (participating in) 1,100 funerals you become very cold, unemotional, but this situation was a little different."

In Dallas, Gov. Connally is watching the funeral on the television set in his Parkland hospital room.

The Dallas Morning News

Fellow Dallas police officers carry the coffin of officer J.D. Tippit at Laurel Land Memorial Park.

The Dallas Morning News

A Dallas police officer escorts J.D. Tippit's widow, Marie, at his funeral.

Connally: "It was strange, almost as if I was in a dream. I think I was still probably fairly highly sedated, but I remember it extremely well.

"It had an unrealistic quality about it to me because the last time I had been conscious, we were riding together in a car and then, as I regained consciousness briefly on Sunday, Nellie told me, confirmed, that the president had been fatally wounded."

2 p.m.

In Dallas, the funeral service for officer Tippit starts at Beckley Hills Baptist Church, with the Rev. Tipps presiding.

Tipps: "He was doing his duty when he was taken by the lethal bullet of a poor, confused, misguided, ungodly assassin — as was our president."

Thousands have gathered for the service. Afterward, Tippit will become the first person to be buried in a special section at Laurel Land Memorial Park for those who gave their lives in community service.

Tipps: "It was on television and reporters were there. Sometimes they were kind of rude. Like when the coffin was being transported, conduct wasn't like it ought to be.

"I was just trying to help the family. She (Mrs. Tippit) was a very quiet lady, and she really had a struggle because she was alone. She said she didn't think she could have made it if it hadn't been for her faith in the Lord.

"There were about 5,000 to 6,000 people at the funeral service. Since the church sat on about 20 acres of land, it was easy to accommodate that many people....A lot didn't even know the family, but they just came out because they'd heard about it.

"I remember that I tried not to be lengthy (in the sermon)....It was only about 15 or 20 minutes. The message that God had promised us eternal life. When a person is a Christian his body may die but spiritually live with the Lord forever.

"I really feel like we were able to help her."

Marie Tippit's brother, Dwight Gasway, is moved by the 700 police officers who attend the funeral.

Gasway: "I remember thinking…that it was great. I kept thinking that it was the most law enforcement officers I had seen at one time in my life."

As the Tippit service is held, preparations for the Oswald funeral still have not been finalized. The Secret Service finally tells Gaertner that arrangements have been made with another minister.

Gaertner: "But the other minister (a Lutheran, Paul Frank) — when he called the funeral home, he was told that he didn't have to go, that I was going."

Because of the confusion, neither minister will show up at Rose Hill Cemetery later that afternoon.

2:07 to 2:08 p.m.

Taps is played at Arlington, and the bugler, Clark, misses a note.

Post engineer Carroll: "You hate to see something like that for a great man to go wrong. You don't want anything to go wrong....

"And the only thing that happened was that the bugler who played taps missed one note, and it was kind of obvious. But shoot, I would have too if I had been him. I would have been pretty nervous."

Clark: "In the normal course of standing there for three hours and not being able to touch the instrument — normally you need a little time to warm up, but you can't do that at the cemetery — there was a little fluke on the third note....It just happened....

"I believe it was *Newsweek* that picked it up. They called it a tear within the music of playing the taps. But I didn't make any comment on that. If they want to say that, it was fine."

2:08 to 2:12 p.m.

The coffin team folds the flag that had been draped over the coffin and hands it to Metzler. The Marines play Eternal Father. *Cushing blesses the torch for the eternal flame, and Metzler gives the flag to Mrs. Kennedy.*

Lyndon Johnson: "We stood in chill and silence for the final firing of salute and the folding of the flag."

2:13 p.m.

Mrs. Kennedy lights the eternal flame. The flame is fueled by bottled gas that engineer Carroll has hidden behind a nearby rock.

Carroll: "I was standing behind the major of the 3rd Infantry. I had a little glass of kerosene into which I dipped the taper, and I handed it to him, and he took his cigarette lighter and lit it and put it in the hand of Mrs. Kennedy and guided her hand to the flame. And I signaled the man over under the trees to turn the valve on (the bottled gas) and the taper lit the flame.

"It worked like clockwork."

About 2:15 p.m.

The service ends. John Connally III, standing with the Johnsons, has a letter for Mrs. Kennedy from his mother.

Connally: "We walked down from grave site to limousine, and Jackie

Jacqueline Kennedy holds the flag that covered her husband's coffin.

Associated Press

Kennedy and Robert Kennedy jumped out when President Johnson walked up. He expressed his condolences and then introduced me....

"I shook hands with Robert Kennedy. He was very shaken, as we all were. He just nodded and said hello. Of course I didn't know what to say either.

"And then the president introduced me to Mrs. Kennedy. I expressed my sympathy. She just hung on to my hand,

just kept kind of clutching my hand. And she said, 'I hope you'll tell your mother I'm so glad your father will be OK. That's the only good thing to come out of this.'

"She still had on the black veil and there were tears still on it.

"She kept clutching my hand, and I couldn't reach into my pocket. I wanted to give her the note from my mother. It was in the right pocket of my overcoat

UPI/Bettmann Newsphotos

Jacqueline Kennedy clasps the hand of Robert Kennedy.

and she had my right hand. I had to do it left-handed."

The crowd begins to disperse.

Kilduff: "Everyone just quietly drifted away."

Sen. Yarborough: "As the crowd fell away, I walked up to the grave....I was thinking of Kennedy and the loss to the world. It's an unspeakable tragedy for any president to be assassinated. Aside from that family, it was a loss to the whole world. He was a hero to the whole world. People cried in every nation when he died."

2:34 p.m.

Electric power to the cemetery is cut off as the lowering device begins to let down the coffin.

Miller: "They were getting ready to lower the coffin into the grave, but the TV networks wouldn't shut down their cameras and leave. At the time, the cameras ran off electricity rather than batteries like they do now.

"We didn't want it filmed. That's not necessary....(But) they wouldn't turn them off, so Metzler finally told the post engineer to turn off the electricity.

"Then they packed up and left and he lowered the coffin into the vault."

Metzler: "We were going to lower the coffin into the ground, and I saw no reason why the ghouls should be making a picture of that, and I cut the juice off in the stands."

After 2:30 p.m.

At the White House, Mrs. Kennedy is receiving heads of state and other dignitaries who attended the funeral.

Duke: "We went straight from Arlington to the White House. Mrs. Kennedy had gone ahead. We came in the diplomatic entrance and we went upstairs, and I formed a receiving line in the Red Room. I stood at her side and I introduced the first guest, and the others quickly came along.…

"It was quite a group and she was absolutely superb. To each one of them she had something to say. It was extraordinary.…

"Mrs. Kennedy had been concerned in the early days about this business of curtsying… and I told her no, there is no curtsying when you are of equal rank. She understood the logic of it.

"And when the Duke of Edinburgh came through the line, she curtsied to him, and then she turned to me and she said, 'You see, I'm not the wife of a chief of state anymore.'

"And there were tears streaming down my cheeks. It was quite a statement."

Powers: "President (Eamon) de Valera (of Ireland) had gone up to see Jackie, and then he came back down. This man who represented so much of Ireland's history, and he sat there, sobbing, in the Cabinet room of the White House.…

"He said, in Ireland historians would compare the tragic death of John Kennedy to one of Ireland's own great liberators, Owen Roe O'Neill, and he quoted a poem Thomas Davis wrote, something about sheep without a shepherd, why did you leave us, why did you die? And he sobbed."

About 3 p.m.

In Dallas, Marguerite and Marina Oswald are getting ready for Lee Harvey Oswald's funeral.

Marguerite Oswald: "Marina was very unhappy with the dress — they bought her two dresses. 'Mama, too long.' 'Mama, no fit.' And it looked lovely on her.

"I said, 'Oh, honey, put your coat on, we are going to Lee's funeral. It will be all right.'"

About 3:30 p.m.

Metzler escorts the last of the prominent

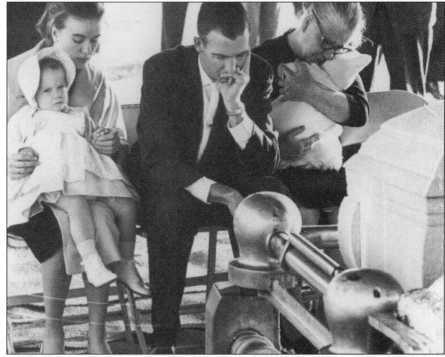

Associated Press

Marina Oswald (left) holds her daughter June Lee at a simple funeral for Lee Harvey Oswald at Rose Hill Cemetery in Fort Worth. With her are Robert Oswald and Marguerite Oswald, holding Marina's other daughter, Rachel.

guests from the burial site and then sees Sgt. Maj. Frank Ruddy walk up to the grave.

Metzler: "A man came back and put his green beret down on the shrubbery around the eternal flame, and everybody did the same…the other branches of service."

Between 3:30 and 4 p.m.

Saunders, of the Fort Worth Area Council of Churches, is still uncomfortable with the arrangements for Oswald's funeral. He drives to Rose Hill Cemetery, where the burial is scheduled for 4 p.m. He realizes that no other ministers have shown up. Funeral home director Groody asks him to perform the service.

Saunders: "I don't believe I've ever had a more difficult moment.…I hadn't had a funeral in quite some time. I had become an administrator.…

"With reluctance and yet a sense of responsibility, I walked over to Mrs. (Marguerite) Oswald and asked her,

'What are your wishes?' She said she'd like for me to have the burial service for her son.…

"I asked her to tell me something about him. She said he was a good son, a good husband and a good father.…

"I had an awareness that anything I said (because of the extensive media coverage) could be evaluated, misinterpreted or misunderstood.…I recognized this could be an international incident.

"I felt that whatever happened could be seen as a reflection of the church's feeling and understanding of what this family was going through. I felt I had to express a deep-seated concern of Christian faith for a family in trouble."

About 4 p.m.

At Rose Hill, a group of reporters, including The Associated Press' Cochran, is asked to carry Oswald's coffin from the chapel to the grave site because no arrangements had been made for pallbearers.

Cochran: "I think I was offended at the prospect of carrying the coffin. But when Preston McGraw of UPI was recruited and he said he'd do it, I think I felt it was my duty to carry it for AP.

"There was also in the back of my mind, I guess I was thinking that if we didn't do it, that if we didn't get this guy buried...we wouldn't be able to file our stories, that the sooner he was buried, the sooner we'd file the story and I could get to watch some of what was going on in Washington.

"You can imagine it (the service) was somber. I think the only ones there were the brother, Robert, and Marina, with the two little girls and Marguerite. It was a grim affair...just a handful of family and a whole slew of reporters.

"I can assure you I had no sense of history that day. It was a story and an unpleasant story at the scene of a very unpleasant news event."

Saunders: "I made a brief statement to the effect that we were here to lay away Lee Harvey Oswald, not judge him. I quoted from memory the 23rd Psalm and the 14th Chapter of John. I prayed that the love of God, who we know through Jesus Christ, might comfort the mother and family in that dark and tragic moment.

"There was a dim awareness in me of the tremendous contrast between the beautiful and carefully worked-out service for President Kennedy and the very humble and stark service we were having (for Oswald)....

"The service itself probably took about 10 minutes. The family left very quickly after it was over."

After 4 p.m.

In Washington, Johnson is hosting a reception for foreign dignitaries at the State Department.

Duke: "At one point all the kings of Scandinavia, and the presidents of Finland and Iceland, had a little caucus and were sitting in a circle of sofas at the end of the room, and Johnson came over and joined them.

"At that time, President de Gaulle came in downstairs...and he asked where President Johnson was, and as he came over they all stood up and he stretched out his arms, it looked like he was about to knock them all down, to embrace President Johnson, which was quite a dramatic thing."

At Arlington National Cemetery, the body bearers are relieved of duty.

Cheek: "After the funeral, that was probably when everything started to hit us. We got in the bus and went back to Army barracks and dispersed from there. That was the first time we didn't have anything to face us the next day.

"Initially we were all pretty quiet, we were in a state of disbelief as to what had happened. Then we started talking about it."

Felder: "We stayed there until all the crowds had gone, and we initially provided a cordon, security, until they could provide some relief for us. Then I went back to the barracks, changed my clothes and went home.

"I sat down in my living room and all of a sudden I couldn't hold it, I just cried, boo-hooed. All of a sudden it hit me what I had done that day as I was watching the TV reruns."

6 p.m.

After the receptions, close friends and family members gather at the White House to comfort Mrs. Kennedy — and to observe her son's birthday.

Powers: "John was well aware it was his birthday. His father had told him he would bring him something, and a 3-year-old boy just knows it's his birthday. Jackie and Lee (Radziwill, Jacqueline's sister) and Bobby Kennedy and I were there, and we sang *Happy Birthday* and John had a cake.

"It must have been the saddest *Happy Birthday* ever sung....But we smiled at John, being that happy. We all put on an act."

7:32 p.m.

Johnson, meeting with the governors of 30 states, says that he will press for enactment of a tax cut and civil rights legislation proposed by Kennedy and that he'll begin that push in a speech to Congress on Wednesday night.

Johnson: "(I told them,) 'We are going to have plenty of time after the conventions to get out and campaign and talk about ourselves and our merits. Let's talk about our country until then and let's not just talk about it, but let's get some action on it and do something....

"'We have hate abroad in the world, hate internationally, hate domestically where a president is assassinated and then they (the haters) take the law into their own hands and kill the assassin. That is not our system.'"

Johnson aide Valenti: "Everything he was doing in those first days was part of his grand design to allay fears....He had to demonstrate the government was in strong hands, unhesitant hands.

"That was his main goal that first week, to ease the anxieties around the country and the world...and to show the linkage between the 35th and 36th president."

About 11 p.m.

Jacqueline and Robert Kennedy decide to make another visit to Arlington cemetery.

Metzler: "That night I got a call at 11 o'clock and Robert and Jackie came over, and they knelt down, said their prayers."

As the clocks strike midnight, Mrs. Kennedy lays a bouquet of lilies of the valley on the grave, and she and her brother-in-law walk quietly away.

In the next few days, Mrs. Kennedy will return several times to the grave site. And in the months and years to follow, hundreds of thousands of others will also come to pay their respects to the slain president — to gaze at the flicker of the eternal flame, and to wonder what might have been.

SHADOWS

Dallas' Dark Journey

An essay by Blackie Sherrod

First of all, you must realize that the press box is the Plymouth Rock for all gallows humor as we know it today. There is no subject sacred to the biting lash of the sports authors, not so much in their literary efforts but in their personal communication. Believe me, the press box was spewing sick humor around long before cable television.

And just as the wretches strive for toppers, also are they dedicated to stoicism. If a barb lodges under one's skin, one must never show it. One must be as the Spartan child who stole a fox, hid it under his tunic and when it began gnawing on his flesh, never changed expression lest it would give away his crime.

Those were the accepted press box mores in December 1963 when I walked into a hospitality suite at the Lexington Hotel in Manhattan. It was a sports trip, a gathering of All-America footballers and attending writers.

"Watch out, everybody!" yelled a man at the bar. "Here's that guy from Dallas! He's probably got a gun!"

The joker was an old newspaper pal from Georgia. The accepted reaction would have been to crouch at the knees, slap the hip in a swift draw. Instead, I got mad. Well, not exactly mad, but I felt a quick surge of resentment toward my old friend. I felt my ears turning crimson, could actually feel the heat.

The sense of dark humor had taken a leave of absence. I was utterly defenseless and I didn't like the feeling; I wanted to strike back but didn't know how. I felt ashamed and yet I was angry at myself for that feeling.

Now, looking back on those bewildering times, I realize that must have

---

We were the mother whose beloved son has been caught in the act of armed robbery. What can you say?

---

been the prevalent emotion that gripped the city in the immediate days after the assassination of President John F. Kennedy on that damned miserable Nov. 22. Residents of Dallas, at least the overwhelming majority, were saddened by the rifle shots, certainly, but down deep inside, we also were resentful as hell that it happened here. Perhaps civic loyalists have a difficult time admitting that even today, but that's the way it was.

You see, this was new to the world. Today, cities could handle it. Today, people are hardened to sudden changes of history. We are still shocked but the recovery time is far less. Forces go into immediate action and confusion is cut to a minimum, like grammar school pupils in a well-disciplined fire drill. Back then, it was a stunner. It was like Joe Louis banging you on the chin and, even if you didn't lose consciousness, you felt powerless to move. You could see and hear and smell, but you were maddeningly immobile.

Oh, proud Dallas historians might have you think the city rallied around, that astute leaders mounted their chargers and quickly began positive moves.

Not from where I sat, there in the newsroom of an afternoon paper.

It seemed to me that the brave, resolute commanders — and even many of us enlisted men — jutted our stalwart jaws, sprang to the saddle and rode determinedly off in all directions. We wanted desperately to defend the fort but we didn't know the drill. We were the mother whose beloved son has been caught in the act of armed robbery. What can you say?

It was like menfolk at an old-timey country funeral. Women busied themselves inside the house, answering the phone, slicing the baked ham, tending

---

The Texas School Book Depository window from which Lee Harvey Oswald is said to have fired the shots that killed the president.

the mourners. And the men gathered awkwardly in the yard, smoking, uncomfortable in starched collars and small talk. And a lady would call from the back porch, asking someone to fetch bread from the grocery and a dozen men would jump for their cars. They wanted action, wanted movement, wanted to demonstrate by their energies that they could be of use, could contribute to easing the day.

That's the way I remember that assassination aftermath. Nobody wanted to stand around and talk about it; everybody wanted to do something. It wasn't always the right thing. Nobody was real sure of the route to the grocery store. Those in the media were more fortunate than others. They stayed busy. Yet frequently they stepped out of character. I remember standing in the editor's office (watching the only television set on the floor), reporters sitting on the carpet, leaning against the wall, when the announcer gave the definite news that the president indeed was dead. I heard a gasp and a male reporter was sobbing. I had never seen that before.

Late the next night, those on the midnight watch heard fearful screams from somewhere down the corridors. Understand, the assassination brought nuts out of the woodwork like earthworms after a rain. We had zany newsroom visitors who shouted and threatened and had to be removed forcibly. So screams in the night were not exactly out of mode.

Reporters scattered at high lope, each seeking the source. Finally it was traced. A veteran pressman was trapped on stairs between floors. The door he entered locked behind him, the door he sought

was locked in front of him. So he screamed at the top of his voice, really terrified shrieks. A week earlier, he would never have done that. A week later, it would have embarrassed him to tears. But now, when the door was opened to free him, he said not a word, just walked off to his pressroom station.

Merriman Smith, the senior White House correspondent, came to our office to write and file his assassination coverage for United Press International. He was a calm white-haired professional and it was most impressive when he finished, boarded the elevator and said, as the door closed, "Big D is Little D now."

Those who heard him resented it, mostly because we feared that would be the international opinion. Yet some of us have long held the theory that Jack Ruby's shooting of Lee Harvey Oswald — more than the assassination — was the absolute crusher for the Dallas image, if we may call it that.

On Sunday in Washington, the riderless horse and the muffled drums (you would never, never forget that drum beat) were bearing the president's coffin to the Capitol. And in the basement of the City Hall and police buildings, Ruby was shooting Oswald in the left side with a .38-caliber Colt. Were it not for Ruby's act, the assassination might not have been so damning for the city. The town might have escaped as "a victim of circumstance," like Buffalo, N.Y., where William McKinley went down and the Washington depot where James Garfield was shot, mere happenstance locations that did not add to nor subtract from the happening itself.

But then the Ruby slaying pulled the plug. In the City Hall basement, can you believe it! This became the Dallas black eye that no amount of brave cosmetics could disguise. And to compound it all, the mystery of Oswald died with him and the speculation kept, and still keeps, the subject dreadfully alive.

I remember an FBI agent, a friend of mine, coming to the newspaper office late Friday night of the assassination, to inspect all photographs shot by our lensmen that day, seeking any background face or anything that might be a clue as to Oswald's motive. He cursed Oswald, looked over his shoulder and muttered confidentially.

"I wish they'd let us have him for a few hours," he said. "We'd shoot his ass full of sodium pentothal and find out what's going on."

Instead the question remains in history, like the hulk of the USS Arizona in the shallow waters of Pearl Harbor, oil still seeping to the surface, a subject to be brought down from the shelf and dusted and polished every decade or so.

To Dallas old-timers, the tragedy has become like a birthmark on your child's face. The blemish is there but you have become accustomed to it so that it is no longer a constant heartache. Not until a stranger remarks about it, that is, not until you drive past the old School Book Depository and see tourists staring at the sixth-floor window and unstrapping their Kodaks. And you still feel, however faintly, that stir of resentment and you realize again that the day and its shadow will never be forever erased from memory.

HAS DALLAS CHANGED?

Commentary

By Stanley Marcus

For months I had been able to foresee the deluge of writers, reporters, photographers and all kinds of electronic-media journalists from America and other parts of the world flooding in on Dallas on the occasion of another anniversary of the assassination of President John F. Kennedy. Immediately after that event I was eager to talk about it, but as the years have passed, I find myself less desirous of discussing the subject and even hostile at times to those new-generation reporters who feel confident of their ability to dig out the real story that their predecessors missed.

Thus, I found it refreshing to be writing about it instead of talking about it. I presume that there is a lingering suspicion that the real assassin was never identified and that vows of silence possibly organized by the local population will eventually crack apart, revealing hitherto undisclosed clues. Europeans never bought the idea that the murder was the work of a loner rather than of a conspiracy involving multinational agents.

The question most frequently posed to me by journalists is, "Has Dallas changed since Nov. 22, 1963?" My reply usually is, "Why should it have changed?" or, "Every city changes in 25 years, for change is the most constant factor in life." What they really mean is, "Did the assassination force noticeable changes in Dallas institutions and on the populace as a whole?"

Visitors, as well as a large portion of the population, fail to understand that Dallas is very conservative politically and that it has been so for a good number of years. In the 1920s, one did not have to be a Republican to be conservative in Dallas. One simply voted the Democratic ticket, for in this part of America the Democratic Party was conservative. Dallas County elected Hatton Sumners to Congress from

---

...it takes more than an assassination to change the course of human nature.

1913 to 1947, creating a seniority that earned him the chairmanship of the House Judiciary Committee.

With the Depression and the election of Franklin Roosevelt to the presidency, Dallasites had their first exposure to a more liberal political philosophy, and they didn't like it. Other sections of the state with larger numbers of blue-collar workers supported Roosevelt with enthusiasm,

but not Dallas. This observation is made not in criticism but rather in recognition of the historical attitude of the city and the county.

In the second and third decades of the century, the economy of Dallas was based on agriculture, cotton in particular, with its attendant businesses, such as ginning, warehousing, compressing and shipping. Cattle ranching ranked as a poor second. Dallas became a center for the insurance industry and for wholesale and retail distribution. Unionism was discouraged and Dallas, in fact, proudly proclaimed itself an "open shop" city. When oil roared in during the '30s, its producers, for the most part, became rich conservatives.

The economic makeup of the city either attracted a conservative press or encouraged one. *The Dallas Morning News* became ultraconservative under the publishing direction of Ted Dealey. The *Dallas Times Herald* maintained a moderately conservative stance and the only liberal sheet in town, the *Dallas Dispatch*, struggled for years and finally died in 1942 for lack of both reader and advertising support.

Lyndon Johnson was never popular in Dallas; he was a new breed of politician that the Dallas business leadership didn't care for. Johnson was regarded as a liberal, one who advocated social change, a philosophy for which the conservative leadership of Dallas was not ready. It could not see beyond its own range of self-interest, and it refused to enhance its vision by using a magnifying glass to enlarge its

The Dallas Morning News

Dallas in 1993: A city grappling with many critical issues, but none related to the death of Kennedy.

ability to look into the future. When Kennedy came to Texas to campaign, he was rejected by the Dallas establishment because of his advocacy of social change. This was a much stronger negative than the fact that he was a Catholic. The upper-middle-class social structure was prosperous and happy with the status quo, and it didn't like Kennedy, whom it regarded as a threat to its well-being. It was doing well, and it didn't want change.

Conservative as the business leadership was, it was middle-of-the-road in its attitudes as compared with a small group of articulate far-righters. It was the far-right lunatic fringe that paid for the anti-Kennedy advertisement that appeared in *The Dallas Morning News* on Nov. 22, the day of Kennedy's visit, and who circulated the "Wanted for Treason" handbills.

The failure of the middle-of-the-road conservative majority was that it hadn't acted in protest at an earlier date — not just a day or two prior to the president's visit, but months before when a state of absolutism reigned supreme in the city. That was when the leaders should have acted but didn't. Leadership in Dallas did not lead; it did not rise to the challenge.

The vice president had called me from Washington to announce that President Kennedy had decided to make a trip to Texas. Johnson wanted me to raise money for a proper reception and entertainment for the president. After the raucous and rude treatment given to Adlai Stevenson the previous month, I feared that Kennedy might be subjected to similar embarrassment, so I urged Johnson to discourage him from coming to Dallas.

Johnson's reply was curt. "What you think and what I think isn't worth a damn. Kennedy has decided that he is coming. Now, go out and raise the money!" As a dutiful foot soldier, I complied with his directions. Although I feared inhospitable demonstrations, at no time did I conceive that the president might be physically attacked.

The international community that had become used to assassinations and terrorism shuddered and agonized over Kennedy's death. National and world opinion turned against Dallas, which some writers labeled as "the city of hate." A world that had accepted the horrors of the Holocaust with placidity burst out indignantly against Dallas, threatening boycott and retaliation. The Dallas citizenship was mortified, the political minority that had supported Kennedy was grief-stricken, the leadership was numb and indecisive in trying to formulate a plan of action to re-establish the dignity and position of the city. Countless meetings were held that resulted in few decisions of importance. The one good conclusion was to refuse the suggestion that the city should employ a public relations firm to try to repair the damaged reputation of Dallas.

What had gone wrong? A large portion of the local citizenship resented the charges that were being leveled at Dallas. "This could have happened anywhere. Dallas should not be blamed for the act of a single assassin or even of a group of killers." That sense of resentment still exists and was probably responsible, in part, for the lack of local financial support for the long-delayed Kennedy exhibit.

Dallas had no tradition of pluralism; it was pretty much a mind-set community that did not welcome differences in opinion. In this regard it differed from such cities as conservative Boston, integrated Atlanta or liberal Portland, Ore.

Though the leadership was justified, in my opinion, for rejecting the broad charges made against the city, the more moderate forces in the religious, educational and business leadership of the community had been reluctant to vigorously protest the activities of the far right, thus, in a way, giving sanction to their acts of extremism. This group failed to stand up for free expression, it failed to vigorously oppose the spirit of absolutism that dominated the city for a half-dozen years.

What happened as a result? Did the world boycott Dallas? Did new business organizations refuse to move to the city? Did individuals carry out threats that they wouldn't come to Dallas to live? The growth records of the succeeding years suggest that the answer is a resounding "no" to all of these questions.

Dallas has had an unprecedented physical and financial growth in the past two decades. Its economy is now struggling but not as a result of the assassination. A few changes for the better have occurred. Pluralism, the acceptance of differences in opinions, has gained respectability, encouraged, no doubt, by the dramatic changes in direction that occurred in *The Dallas Morning News*, which, in the intervening years, has shifted from the far right in its editorial direction to a middle-of-the-road type of conservatism.

The fact that Dallas public opinion has become more fair and tolerant than previously can be attributed to the deliberate effort of *The News* to present deeper and more diverse news coverage and a balanced set of opinions on controversial subjects. Part of this change must also be credited to the thousands of immigrants from other states who have made Dallas their home. They represent the spectra of opinions, and they have helped water down the prior extremism.

In the '40s and '50s the city had been under the strong influence of the Dallas Citizens Council, a group of business leaders who exercised a beneficent influence over political, educational and cultural affairs. It wasn't very democratic, but it was very effective in steering the activities of the city toward growth and national importance. It became one of the casualties of the post-assassination period. The "Oligarchy," a tag hung on it by the press, felt obliged to modify its leadership in response to the implied criticism of its active role. The organization continues to operate but with considerably less vigor and sense of purpose.

Where do we go from here? Dallas has a long way to go to solve its problems of Balkanization, to provide for racial and minority inequities, to demonstrate a determination to act instead of talk about its transportation crisis. However, none of these critical issues are related to the death of Kennedy. These are problems that we as citizens have refused to give the priority they require. There may be some who think we can continue to ignore them and that they will go away, but that's not how great cities are built.

We did not listen to Kennedy's goals while he was alive; we don't remember them now. The assassination did not lead, as many had hoped, to the transformation of Dallas to a city of brotherly love. There is little evidence to prove that Dallasites are more or less humane, more or less interested in the welfare of their fellow citizens. They preach democracy to the world but resent democracy in action when some of the elected minority leaders use shrill and abrasive techniques to register their opinions. The courts have been more responsible than the electorate in making the city and its institutions practice democratic procedures, leading to the inevitable conclusion that it takes more than an assassination to change the course of human nature.

Stanley Marcus is chairman emeritus of Neiman Marcus and a marketing consultant. Marcus, whose father, aunt and uncle founded Neiman Marcus in 1907, has been in the retailing business for more than 60 years.

LEE HARVEY OSWALD

A Life Without an Anchor

By Bill Minutaglio

A young reporter, Priscilla Johnson of the North American Newspaper Alliance, entered the American Embassy in Moscow on the afternoon of Nov. 16, 1959. The embassy was where journalists picked up their mail.

As Ms. Johnson walked through the embassy, she was approached by John McVickar, a senior consular officer. "There is an American staying in your hotel who says he wants to defect," said the gruff-voiced McVickar. "He says he won't talk to any of us. But maybe he will talk to you because you are a woman."

Ms. Johnson knew full well that at the time, ties between the United States and the Soviet Union were mired in a crucial, tender state. She also was aware that the rare defector could mutate into a high-profile pawn, someone who could be manipulated by either country. She quickly returned to her hotel, a Spartan outpost for foreigners called The Hotel Metropole.

She went directly to the second floor, where she had been told the defector was staying.

Ms. Johnson knocked on a door. It opened a crack. Lee Harvey Oswald stared back at her.

Oswald kept his foot firmly planted in the doorway, blocking her view and her possible entry into his room. Reticent, Oswald agreed to visit Ms. Johnson later that evening.

She spent four hours talking to the man who four years later would be charged with killing President John F. Kennedy. The man who, in turn, would be shot and killed almost 48 hours after Kennedy's death. A man whose young life was already a hazy swirl of ambiguity, ambition and jumbled philosophies.

At 9 p.m., Oswald arrived at Ms. Johnson's third-floor residence. She made strong Russian tea on an electric hot plate and poured the beverage into green ceramic mugs. They talked until 1 a.m.

This is her account of the meeting: "I am here because I am a Marxist," Oswald told Ms. Johnson. "For the last two years, I have been wanting to do this one thing.... I spent two years preparing to come here."

Ms. Johnson, who had earned a master's degree in Russian studies at Harvard University, readily grasped that Oswald was unusual. Ideological defections to the Soviet Union were rare through the 1950s.

She also sensed that Oswald, who had just turned 20, was quite lonely. He seemed so collegiate-looking in his dark gray flannel suit, V-neck sweater vest and white shirt with a red tie. Finally, she ascertained that Oswald's mother figured very prominently in his life. She could tell by the way Oswald's voice hardened and grew cold when he mentioned her.

"What does your mother do?" asked Ms. Johnson.

"She is a victim of capitalist society," Oswald dryly replied, his voice dropping a little bit.

Ms. Johnson asked Oswald where he had first heard of communism. Oswald said that he had grown interested after an old woman on a New York street corner handed him literature about Julius and Ethel Rosenberg — the U.S. citizens who were executed after a guilty verdict of conspiracy to commit wartime espionage. There were other stages in his interest:

"At the age of 15, after watching the way workers are treated in New York, and Negroes in the South, I was looking for a key to my environment. Then I discovered socialist literature," Oswald said.

Being a citizen of the United States, "I would become either a worker exploited for capitalist profit, or an exploiter. Or, since there are many in this category, I'd be one of the unemployed."

Ms. Johnson looked intently at Oswald. She saw a pleasant-faced young man captivated by Marxist catch phrases and obsessed with ideology — but not thoroughly understanding of it. A seemingly harmless youngster who had once served in the Marine Corps. A not fully mature man who clearly thought of himself as a loner with an idealistic mission.

"I want to give the people of the United States something to think about," she remembered Oswald saying.

Two days after Oswald left Ms. Johnson's room, she learned that he had disappeared. She had hoped to stay in touch with him, to at least know where he was headed in the Soviet Union.

"I admired his tenacity. He wanted to become a (Soviet) citizen and he wanted to work there. I thought they would send him to a provincial city where there were no foreigners and he would be cut off," says Ms. Johnson.

She says she doubted that this "victim of ignorance" — someone who desperately seemed to believe that the defection of a former Marine would be a heralded political protest — really even knew what it meant to be "a worker."

She thought that he was, perhaps, a perfect product of confused, Cold War times: A man still fathoming and sorting giant political options. Someone inexorably drawn to questions that he believed were beyond the ken of less-driven people.

"I didn't realize how angry he was," says Ms. Johnson. "He was saying, 'I just turn thumbs down on everything, on it all.'"

Later, she would come to believe that Oswald was someone seeking truth in life, someone who wanted answers to vexing questions of inhumanity, injustice, civil rights and freedom.

And only later would she fully appreciate how Oswald's goals, and personality, were driven by his early, unstable and itinerant existence.

By the time he arrived in the Soviet Union in late 1959 — still just a teenager — Oswald's life had been a series of constantly shifting scenarios with few firm friends, few hard-and-fast personal building blocks.

He was born at the Old French Hospital in New Orleans on Oct. 18, 1939. Two months earlier, his father — Robert E. Lee Oswald, named after the Civil War general — had died of a heart attack.

His mother, also born in New Orleans, took tight control of the family. For a good deal of Oswald's life, his mother would remain one of the few fixed, predictable elements of his existence.

He constantly relocated to different homes in New Orleans and even spent time in a children's home while his mother struggled to work. He moved with his mother and her new husband to Fort Worth in the mid-1940s.

The family was splintered by divorce, and Marguerite Oswald moved yet again, this time to a smaller house also in Fort Worth. By the age of 10, Oswald had already attended six schools.

In 1952, Lee and his mother moved to New York to join his older brother, who was stationed there with the Coast Guard. In the next two years there were two apartments, and two schools, which Oswald rarely attended. There were brushes with truant officers, a detention home and a psychiatrist who said Oswald was an intelligent boy who led a "vivid fantasy life."

Oswald and his mother went back to New Orleans in 1954. And if there was

Oswald sits with his wife, Marina, and daughter, June, in the Soviet Union, where the young ex-Marine moved in late 1959.

Lee Harvey Oswald's portrait at age 2.

another constant in his life, aside from his mother and his fascination with Marxism, it would be his attraction to New Orleans.

He spent a total of seven years there, longer than anywhere else he would live. There was a network of cousins, aunts and uncles there, but far beyond the familial bonds, the periods he spent in that complex city had been — and would be — filled with pivotal personal moments:

New Orleans was where the teen-age Oswald extensively nurtured, through hours at the library, his early, budding interest in political philosophies. Later it was where he embarked on his arduous journey to his new home in the Soviet Union. It also was where he began to read extensively about John F. Kennedy.

And in New Orleans, Oswald took his political beliefs to confrontational public arenas — a step on which he embarked only a few weeks before Kennedy's November 1963 visit to Dallas.

But first, there were many more moves: From New Orleans, the family went back to Fort Worth in the summer of 1956. That fall, Oswald enlisted in the Marines. He saw Japan and the

Philippines, studied Russian and wrestled with plans to defect.

In September 1959, he arranged to be discharged to care for his mother. A month later he did defect, beginning his trek to the Soviet Union by boarding a Europe-bound freighter in New Orleans.

He spent time as a factory worker in Minsk, where he met and married a young woman named Marina. But in mid-1962, disillusioned by the bureaucracy, unfulfilled ideals and even the harsh weather, Oswald arranged to return to the United States with his wife and child.

His mother was in Fort Worth and Oswald came to Texas. But it was not long before he returned to New Orleans. There he became convinced that he was a man of social action. A man who could bring about change in the United States.

It was the spring of 1963, and Ruth Paine of Irving found her life tightly bound with the activities of the young Oswald family.

Now, Lee Oswald was on the move again, this time preparing to leave for New Orleans. Mrs. Paine, good-natured and a Quaker, agreed to support the young wife and baby he would temporarily leave behind in Dallas.

Mrs. Paine had met the Oswalds at a party in Dallas in February 1963. Generous to a fault — and interested in learning Russian — Mrs. Paine quickly grew close to Marina, who, through Lee's influence, had learned little English.

In the very small Russian community in Dallas, other people were also drawn to the pleasant, waiflike, 21-year-old Marina. But "that community didn't want to do anything with Oswald himself. The help came purely to Marina," remembers Ilya Mamantov, then a geologist for Sun Oil.

Apparently, even among people who he might have assumed would become close friends, Oswald was not easily accepted. To some he simply seemed cold, brusque and somewhat aloof. Now Lee wanted to leave, perhaps to retreat to a secure place: "He was looking for work, and he had been born there," Mrs.

Paine says of Oswald's decision to once more reside in New Orleans.

Mrs. Paine sensed that there might be some problems between Lee and the pregnant Marina, but she remained convinced that Oswald really was a devoted family man.

"I think he did care. I think Marina and the children were the most important things in his life," says Mrs. Paine.

After two weeks by himself in New Orleans, Oswald called Marina, who was living with Mrs. Paine in Irving. He had found a job as a maintenance man at a coffee company.

Marina was ecstatic. "*Papa nas lubet* — Papa loves us," she shouted to June, their child.

The next day, May 10, 1963, Mrs. Paine was driving her station wagon, with the expectant Marina and the Oswald baby, to New Orleans.

"I knew their place had to be modest. I knew they didn't have much money," says Mrs. Paine. At the apartment Lee had rented on Magazine Street, it was obvious that the Oswalds were short of funds.

It also quickly became apparent that there were serious frustrations eating away at the couple. "I was uncomfortable. They did start to bicker and argue," remembers Mrs. Paine.

There were other frustrations, painful humiliations, for the sensitive Oswald during his five-month stay in New Orleans from the spring into the fall of 1963.

In August, Oswald strolled into a general merchandise store just off Canal,

Lee at age 5 with brothers Robert Oswald (left) and John Pic (right).

near the French Quarter. The store was called Casa Roca. The manager, a Cuban named Carlos Bringuier, was a leader in the anti-Castro exile community.

As Oswald looked at shirts, Bringuier continued his conversation with two other people in the store. "We were talking about Cuba and he started looking around. He gave the impression that he was interested and caught up in the conversation," says Bringuier. "Then he offered his services to me to train Cubans to fight Castro."

The first thought that flashed in Bringuier's mind was that Oswald was an infiltrator — either a Communist or someone from the federal government.

The paranoid, spy-vs.-spy mentality of the era was a firm reality. The U-2 incident, the Bay of Pigs fiasco and the Cuban missile crisis had catapulted already festering fears to new levels.

Bringuier didn't trust the stranger. But Oswald stayed for 45 minutes, convincing Bringuier of his sincerity. "He appeared to be very friendly and very cooperative. He said he knew how to demolish bridges," says Bringuier.

The next day, Oswald returned to the store and dropped off his Marine guidebook. Three days later a friend of Bringuier's stepped off a bus on Canal Street and saw Oswald picketing and handing out pro-Castro literature.

The friend, Celso Hernandez, ran to Bringuier's store, and the two ran back to Canal. "When he saw me, he kind of grinned and smiled. He offered to shake hands," says Bringuier. Oswald remained calm and passive even though a crowd was gathering and some people were shouting "Go to Russia!" "Go to Cuba!" and "Kill him!"

Hernandez grabbed Oswald's leaflets and tossed them into the air. Bringuier took off his glasses and approached Oswald, ready to strike him. Oswald looked at Bringuier, dropped his arms and said, "OK, Carlos, if you want to hit me, then hit me."

The police arrived. The crowd dispersed, and Oswald and the two Cubans were taken to jail.

As a grade-school student.

Associated Press

New Orleans police Lt. Francis Martello was waiting for Oswald. Martello was working the intelligence beat, and he thought Oswald's shadowy life was worth checking into: "Had I not been in intelligence, I would not have known him from one piece of spaghetti and another."

Martello's mission during his interrogation of Oswald was "to also make a determination if he was going to cause trouble."

The session quickly became a cat-and-mouse affair. Oswald was cool, almost friendly. He had on a casual summer shirt. The conversation was carefully breezy.

"It was a game. I played mine, and he played his," says Martello, comparing his meeting with Oswald to a class in logic. "I guess he won the first round. I didn't get anything."

But near the end of their encounter, the men were dipping into bigger political issues and ideas. "If you don't like America, where would you hold your loyalty?" Martello remembers asking.

"At the foot of democracy," Oswald said.

Carlos Bringuier recalls that on the day of his trial, Oswald walked into the Southern courtroom and settled on the side where blacks sat. For his role in

disturbing the peace on Canal Street, Oswald was given a $10 fine.

A few days later, Bringuier and the other anti-Castro Cubans decided to infiltrate Oswald's world. The fliers that Oswald had handed out listed his address on Magazine Street.

Carlos Quiroga, an engineer fluent in English, was picked to be the mole. He knocked on the door of Oswald's modest place. "I'm interested in your organization," said Quiroga, referring to the Fair Play for Cuba group that Oswald was promoting.

Oswald, in a T-shirt, sat with Quiroga on the porch. The men talked for 45 minutes. Quiroga was shocked when a small child, June, came out and spoke Russian to her father. Oswald gave Quiroga a booklet and an application form. Oswald talked in depth, convincingly, about his version of Marxism.

"What impressed me the most was the way he talked about his ideas," said Quiroga. "I was also inclined to think that he was a loner." After Quiroga left, he informed the police of his meeting with Oswald.

Meanwhile, the local news media were beginning to take an interest in the unsettled relationship between the Cubans and Oswald — and a radio station set up a debate program. Oswald and Bringuier were invited.

Just before the taping, Bringuier decided to approach Oswald. "No matter that we have disagreements and that you think something and I think something else," said Bringuier. "Any time you change your mind you are free to become my friend and I will help you any way I can."

Oswald, cool and a bit cynical, turned to Bringuier: "I know that I am on the right side."

A few weeks later Oswald moved back to Dallas. In between he made a fruitless trip to Mexico, hoping to persuade the Cuban Embassy there to allow him into Cuba.

Oswald carried along his family's problems. Marina lived with Mrs. Paine in Irving. Lee settled into a furnished

In the Marines at age 19.

Holmes readily agreed. The interview began after Oswald was assured that the stranger in the room, Holmes, was not an FBI agent.

"He wasn't any dummy," says Holmes. "He had pretty good control of himself. He was calm and polite as could be."

At one point, Holmes remembers asking Oswald: "Do you have any religion?"

Oswald answered, "Yeah, I have religion."

Holmes said, "Good, what's your faith?" Oswald simply replied, "Karl Marx."

It would be one of the last conversations Oswald ever had. He was killed a few minutes later.

Today Holmes remains convinced of one thing.

Lee Harvey Oswald, who lived a life without easy answers, would probably never have offered up clear truths: "I got the impression he would never have confessed to anything."

room in Oak Cliff and took a job at the Texas School Book Depository.

New Orleans had not been as fulfilling as he expected. His last extended stay there had been filled with personal attacks, paranoia and a stumbling political agenda.

By the time Lee had left there at the end of September 1963 — almost two months to the day before President Kennedy was killed — it seemed he had left a city that had, perhaps for the first time, joined the ranks of all those who had turned their backs on him.

On Nov. 24, 1963, shortly before 11 a.m., Harry Holmes was sitting across a table from the man many of the people in the room thought had killed President Kennedy two days earlier. Holmes hadn't expected to be there; he was a local postal inspector who had been assisting in tracking down postal boxes, money orders and signatures.

Holmes had dropped his family at church on this Sunday morning and then gone down to the Dallas Police Department to see whether he could help. Capt. Will Fritz appeared in a hallway and, without warning, invited Holmes to join him and Secret Service agents for an interview session with the prisoner.

With Marina shortly after their arrival in Dallas.

JACK RUBY

Obsessions and Contradictions

By Barry Boesch

Jack Ruby's Carousel Club stood on the fringes of Commerce Street's glittering nightclub scene in the early 1960s.

No matter how many mentions he coaxed out of the local columnists, no matter how many free passes he handed out to influential people, Ruby and his burlesque club were destined to remain in the shadows of the more famous Colony Club and the grander showrooms of the Adolphus, Baker and Hilton hotels.

Ruby eventually would get his recognition by a shorter, more tragic route.

On Sunday morning, Nov. 24, 1963, he walked into the basement of the Dallas police station, lunged through a tight throng of detectives and newspeople and shot Lee Harvey Oswald. That act earned him a place in history as the man who killed the man accused of assassinating President John F. Kennedy.

At his trial, prosecutors portrayed Ruby as a cynical, small-time mercenary out for recognition and a little publicity for his nightclub.

Defense attorneys would argue that Ruby was grief-stricken by the assassination, and that his fragile emotional state was further agitated by Oswald's cockiness. They said the moment's intensity triggered a seizure of psychomotor epilepsy, leaving Ruby temporarily insane.

A third, darker portrait of Ruby — that painted by researchers and authors who attribute Kennedy's slaying to a conspiracy — is that the paunchy, enigmatic club owner was a ruthless minion of organized crime.

Ruby told police, his family and friends that he shot Oswald for "Jackie and the kids," to spare them the agony of a trial.

"He told me he thought he was going to be a hero," said Breck Wall, creator of the ribald *Bottoms Up* revue and a friend of Ruby's. "But it backfired, and instead of being a hero, he realized the public was very upset with him."

To many who knew him, that was Jack Ruby — always trying to please, to win acceptance, to succeed — and always falling short.

Jacob Rubenstein grew up in a tough neighborhood on Chicago's West Side, the fifth of eight children, born to immigrant parents on March 25, 1911.

His father was a domineering alcoholic. His mother spent some time in a mental hospital. When he was 11, Jack and his younger brothers and sister were placed in foster homes.

Young Jack, who was known around his neighborhood as "Sparky," had a mercurial temper and was quick with his fists in defense of his siblings.

"He was always highly temperamental. You couldn't insult him," said his younger brother Earl. "He got in a lot of fights. He would just stick up for his rights, like whenever anyone made derogatory remarks about the Jews, or when anybody insulted or annoyed our sisters."

Jack always was devising schemes to make quick money, and not just for himself, said his sister Eva Grant. "During the Depression, I wanted to go to this wedding, but I needed a new dress," Eva said. "Jack went to this wholesale house and got a lot of razor blades. I don't know what he paid for them. He took my sister's card table and went out on the street one Saturday afternoon when a lot of people go out and shop and sold them. He made enough money that at 8 that night, I went into a store and bought a dress for $15."

As a young man, Jack never sought or held a steady job. Instead, he scalped tickets, bought and sold novelty items and knickknacks or solicited newspaper subscriptions.

It was during his teens that Ruby began his association with organized crime by working as a runner for Al Capone. At 25, Ruby worked as a Chicago organizer for the mob-dominated Scrap Iron and Junk Handlers Union.

Ruby's fascination with American presidents surfaced during World War II. After the attack on Pearl Harbor, he sold plaques commemorating the "day of infamy" and busts of Franklin Roosevelt. Fellow soldiers interviewed by the Warren Commission remembered vividly that Ruby wept at the news of Roosevelt's death.

"He had fights about Roosevelt, even Eisenhower, later on," Earl Ruby said.

After the war, he returned to Chicago and with his brothers went into business until 1947, manufacturing small items such as salt and pepper shakers. About that time, Jack and his brothers Earl and Sam had their surname legally changed to Ruby.

In court papers, Jack said most people had come to know him as "Ruby."

Jack soon grew restless. His sister Eva wanted him to come to Dallas to help with her new restaurant-nightclub on South Ervay Street. Eva had come to Dallas a few years earlier as a seller of costume jewelry. She stayed to run the sales division of Southwest Tool and Die.

"Eva had this little restaurant and couldn't run the business herself," Earl said. "We were not making that much money. Jack said since there wasn't enough profit for all of us, he would go down to Dallas and help. I bought him out for about $15,000."

Eva and Jack operated the Singapore Club, which Eva once described as "too nice a club for that part of town."

Eva then moved to San Francisco, and Ruby changed the club's name to the Silver Spur. In early 1949, he signed a young country singer named Dewey Groom. "I made him money," said Groom, the long-time operator of the Longhorn Ballroom before he retired. "He was starving to death when I first met him; we built the place up to turn-away crowds.

"He was cocky, and he had a harem of pretty girls around him. It was prestigious to know Jack Ruby, owner of the Silver Spur."

Groom marveled at Ruby's attempts to save money.

"We worked ungodly hours on Sundays," he said. "To keep us from going out and eating, he would fix us eggs. When he would crack the eggs, he would take a knife and spoon and scrape every drop out of that egg. I couldn't believe that."

Groom became disenchanted when Ruby tried to make the club more than it was. "He started running my people off that weren't dressed to suit him," Groom said. "He wanted to make it an elite Western club. He didn't want people coming in with blue jeans. He was running 'em off faster than I could run 'em in."

Ruby also brought his crime ties to Dallas. Steve Guthrie, Dallas County sheriff in 1947 and 1948, told the FBI in December 1963 that he was told Ruby was a front man for mob interests. "Whenever I wanted to find anyone from the syndicate, I went to Ruby's Silver Spur," Guthrie told federal agents.

Ruby later bought part ownership of the Bob Wills Ranch House, which he held for a short time, and the Vegas Club in Oak Lawn. At the time he shot Oswald, Ruby's only business interests were the Vegas and the Carousel.

While he co-owned the Ranch House, Ruby drew the attention of Tony Zoppi, then a nightclub columnist for *The Dallas Morning News.* "A friend of mine took me there and said, 'There's this character I want you to see,'" Zoppi said. "There was Jack, all decked out in a white cowboy outfit, entertaining and telling jokes. But there were only about seven or eight people in the place.

"Afterward, he came over and said, 'Hi, I'm Jack Ruby from Chicago.' Right away he started dropping names, Irv Kupcinet of the *Chicago Sun-Times* and Dingy Halper, owner of the Chez Paree. I found out later he didn't know these people."

Ruby's bid for the big time came in late 1959. A few doors down from Abe Weinstein's Colony Club, Ruby opened the Sovereign, a richly appointed nightclub requiring a $100 membership fee. He lured Wall's *Bottoms Up* revue from the Adolphus by promising 50 percent of the business to Wall and his partner, Joe Peterson.

The Dallas Morning News

Jack Ruby at the time of his trial in Dallas.

The plan seemed perfect, except no one came. "It just didn't go," Wall said. "After about three months, he changed it to a strip club."

The problem was competition from Weinstein's Colony Club, with its name striptease and musical acts and its more established, high-rolling clientele.

Ruby seemed to try anything to get people into his club. He handed out free passes. Between shows, he raffled off razor blades and turkeys.

"Decor-wise, the Carousel was better than the Colony," said Zoppi. "Business-wise, it couldn't compete. The Colony was established. It drove him crazy."

One time, the Colony had a line around the block waiting to see singer-comedian Rusty Warren. Ruby went up and down the line, beseeching people to come into his place to listen to Rusty Warren records. "I banned him from my club," Weinstein said. "He'd come to my club all the time and try to hire away my waitresses and acts."

Shortly before the assassination, Ruby tried unsuccessfully to have the American Guild of Variety Artists impose sanctions against Weinstein and his brother, Barney, for using nonunion strippers in amateur nights at their clubs.

Newspaper and television reporters in Dallas knew Ruby well.

"He was always looking for a plug in the paper," said Zoppi, who wrote a column called *Dallas After Dark*. "Ruby had an uncanny way of finding out where I was going to have dinner. One time, I was having dinner with Bob Hope, and there was Jack at the next table, staring hard the whole time. Finally, I motioned him over. He handed Hope some free passes and asked him to come to the club."

Behind the tireless promoter was a Jekyll and Hyde. He would slap his sister Eva and later visit her daily in the hospital after an unrelated operation. Shortly before the assassination, he gave a drifter a job and a place to sleep and then fired him for phoning him too early at home.

"He could be your friend one minute and fly off the handle the next," Wall said. "In a matter of one second, he had a row with my partner (Peterson) and threw him down the stairs. Then, when we were in desperate need of money to buy some costumes, he went out and borrowed against his car to give us a loan."

Ruby's personal contradictions also extended to his business. The summer of 1963, trying to boost his business, he hired a flamboyant New Orleans stripper named Jada and paid her double the rate he paid his regular dancers. But then he turned the lights off during her first performance because he objected to the way she pulled on her G-string.

"He couldn't believe she'd done something like that because he wouldn't allow anything like that in our club," said Tammi True, another former Carousel Club stripper. "Also, comedians, when they came in, he would tell them no ethnic jokes, no religious jokes. He didn't want to offend any of the customers in any way," said Miss True, who asked that her real name not be published.

And Ruby still was using his fists to enforce his personal code of honor. Disparaging remarks toward the president, Jews or women often earned a punch in the mouth. "I saw him hit a guy one night for taking advantage of a girl," said Joe Cavagnaro, a friend who worked for Ruby at the Vegas. "He hit the guy clear across the sidewalk."

Ruby was also subject to bouts of severe depression, according to testimony at his trial. Once when one of his clubs failed, Ruby spent two months in a seedy hotel near the Cotton Bowl, emerging only to

Ruby does a turn as a song-and-dance man in Chicago in the late 1950s.

Associated Press

buy groceries. He contemplated suicide several times.

Although his portly physique didn't reflect it, Ruby was health-conscious. He swam, played volleyball at the YMCA, gobbled diet pills and had regular scalp treatments to retard his encroaching baldness.

Beneath Ruby's neatly pressed suit jacket was usually tucked a .38-caliber Colt Cobra he carried for protection. Because of recurring problems with the Internal Revenue Service, he usually carried all his money with him, sometimes as much as several thousand dollars.

He also was a regular hanger-on at the Police Department. Some think he spent time with the police to curry favorable treatment for his club, but others say he genuinely admired and respected the force.

Ruby never married. For years, he dated Alice Nichols, a widow and secretary to an insurance executive. Mrs. Nichols epitomized the class Ruby sought all his life, said Dallas private investigator Bob Denson, who worked for Ruby's defense team during the 1964 trial.

"He was very much in love with her," Cavagnaro said. "He said if he could, he'd marry her tomorrow. But he said he promised his mother on her deathbed that he would never marry out of his religion."

Earl Ruby said his brother also didn't feel financially stable enough to marry. "He said he would not get married until he made it big financially. He made a good living, but he never really made it big."

Ruby kept several dachshunds, which he affectionately called his "wife and children." His favorite dog, Sheba, was with Ruby when he made the drive that took him to his confrontation with Oswald.

Hillel Silverman, who was Ruby's rabbi at Congregation Shearith Israel, remembers a time when Ruby suddenly broke down, weeping and moaning about not having a wife and children.

One of his attorneys, Phil Burleson, said Ruby revered Kennedy not only as the president but also as a father and head of a family. "He had admiration for the president as a man," Burleson said. "Oswald didn't just kill the president. He killed the father of the first family."

Ruby was at *The Dallas Morning News* office placing his weekend advertisements when Kennedy was shot. Later in the afternoon, Ruby called to change the ad to say the Carousel would be closed for the weekend.

Sometime that afternoon, Ruby went to see Cavagnaro at the Hilton.

"He was very, very visibly disturbed," Cavagnaro recalls. "He felt very remorseful for Mrs. Kennedy and the family. He carried on like you would if it were your own cousin or brother."

That night, Ruby went to a memorial service at Shearith Israel. Silverman remembered Ruby sobbing.

Later, Ruby went to the police station with a box full of sandwiches. Because he was a familiar face at headquarters, no one thought it odd that Ruby found his way into a midnight news conference during which police brought Oswald before reporters.

Burleson said it was significant that Ruby saw Oswald and heard District Attorney Henry Wade say that Oswald probably would get the death penalty.

Ruby spent Saturday going around downtown Dallas and back and forth between his Oak Cliff apartment and Eva's apartment. That night, he called Wall in Galveston, complaining that Weinstein had kept the Colony Club open that weekend.

"He was very upset," Wall said. "He didn't think it was right that they didn't close when everything else in Dallas was closed."

On Sunday morning, Ruby was eating breakfast and watching television when one of his strippers, "Little Lynn" Bennett, called him from Fort Worth. Her landlord was threatening to evict her if she didn't pay her rent.

Ruby showered, dressed and picked up his gun. He drove to the Western Union office on Main Street to wire Miss Bennett $25. Ruby then walked one block west to the ramp leading to the Police Department basement.

A police car was getting ready to come up the ramp and turn the wrong way onto Main Street, so patrolman Roy Vaughn —

who was stationed on the ramp — was momentarily distracted. Ruby later said that he walked down the ramp when Vaughn stepped aside for the car, although Vaughn denied that Ruby passed him.

What followed was captured by television and newspaper photographs: Oswald doubled over, shot point-blank in the abdomen by a short, stocky man in a dark suit and snap-brim fedora.

Four minutes after he had wired the money, Ruby was being whisked away to jail and Oswald was bleeding to death on the concrete floor — silenced forever about his role in the president's assassination.

"From what he told me, when he saw Oswald come out with a snicker on his face, seemingly glad about what he'd done, he just lost control," said Earl Ruby.

One day soon after the shooting, Ruby used a phone in the County Jail to call Zoppi, whom he regarded as a friend. Zoppi asked him why he had shot Oswald.

Zoppi recalls: "He started to cry. He said, 'Those poor kids, without a father. I grew up without a father. I know what it's like.' He also said he wanted to save Jackie the embarrassment of having to come down here for the trial."

Jail guards said at the time that Ruby asked over and over: What did the public think? Burleson said that throughout pre-trial preparations, Ruby never seriously believed he could get the death penalty for killing Oswald.

"He was consistent in that he felt Oswald was going to get the death penalty. He was going to die anyway," Burleson said. "Not that he didn't do something wrong, but that the severity of it was not that wrong."

Although Ruby maintained that the shooting of Oswald was not premeditated and not orchestrated by others, his friendships with organized crime figures in Chicago, Dallas, Las Vegas and New Orleans have led many assassination researchers to believe that Ruby acted on orders from mob interests.

Others have described cynical motives for the shooting: "He was going to open a Jack Ruby's on Broadway, write a book, be on TV, be a celebrity, make money," said Dallas lawyer Bill Alexander, one of the team of prosecutors at Ruby's trial.

It wasn't until jury selection was well under way, Burleson said, that Ruby began to realize he might face the electric chair.

"Jack sat there every day listening to people talking about giving him the death penalty," he said. "For a defendant to sit there and listen to that is hard enough. But it was especially hard for a defendant who thought he didn't do anything that bad."

Burleson didn't notice it at the time, but in retrospect, he remembers Ruby slowly becoming more isolated and withdrawn.

Ruby's trial in March 1964 was an international event chronicled by 200 reporters from across the globe. The star of the show was not Ruby but Melvin Belli, the flashy San Francisco trial lawyer whose successes against insurance companies had earned him the sobriquet "King of Torts."

The eight-day trial also featured the salty Alexander, nicknamed "tarantula eyes" by the defense; a pregnant stripper on the witness stand; a jailbreak outside the courtroom; and a protest by epileptic-rights activists.

Belli, sporting Savile Row suits, a black Homburg hat, black boots with 3-inch heels and a purple velvet briefcase, took every opportunity to chasten the judge, the prosecutors — even the city of Dallas.

During the trial, Belli told presiding Judge Joe B. Brown, "You've got blood on your hands." Later, Belli wrote of the trial and Dallas, "Now this self-conscious city had still another act of brutality and anti-intellectual defensiveness to add to its municipal sins."

Belli did not allow Ruby to testify but relied instead on a battery of psychiatric experts to portray Ruby as mentally unstable — volatile, erratic, uncontrollably explosive.

The jury found Ruby guilty of murder and sentenced him to death in the electric chair.

Belli now admits to a few mistakes. "I

Jack Ruby speaks to the press during a break from his 1964 trial for the slaying of Lee Harvey Oswald. Seated at right is defense attorney Melvin Belli.

should have appreciated how proud Dallas was. The first thing I should have done was try to tune in with the Dallas wavelength instead of butting my head against it."

Ruby's other defense attorneys succeeded in 1966 in persuading the Texas Court of Criminal Appeals to overturn the conviction and death sentence, primarily because of Judge Brown's failure to grant a defense request to move the trial from Dallas.

After the trial, Ruby remained in the Dallas County Jail. As his mental health deteriorated, he became convinced that his trial had triggered a pogrom of American Jews by President Lyndon B. Johnson.

"He would claim he could see his brothers Earl and Sam being killed, that they were torturing Eva, that he could see large numbers of Jewish people being massacred," Burleson said.

"He would ask me to get Earl on the phone. Then he began to say, 'That's not Earl. It's someone else.' He finally got to the point that he didn't think I was who I was, face to face."

By the time his conviction and death sentence were overturned and a new trial was ordered, it was too late for Ruby.

"At some point, he lost the desire to live," Burleson said. "I told him that theoretically, he could get out of jail. But he didn't believe it."

On Dec. 9, 1966, Ruby was taken to Parkland Memorial Hospital with a suspected case of pneumonia. Doctors found cancer of the lymph glands.

Ruby died Jan. 3, 1967, barren of the respect and admiration he desired. He was no more than a fringe player in the annals of history.

"Millions of red-blooded Americans wanted to kill Oswald," said his sister Eva.

"Jack was there. That's all."

Staff writers Doug J. Swanson and Steve McGonigle contributed to this report. The article, written for The News' *1983 special report on the Kennedy assassination, was updated in 1988 and 1993.*

JOHN CONNALLY

Texas Governor Carries Doubts About 'Magic Bullets' to the Grave

By Kent Biffle

Three-time Texas Gov. John Bowden Connally carried to his grave an unwavering belief that three shots were fired at the Dallas motorcade on Nov. 22, 1963, each with bloody effect.

The first and third bullets, the governor maintained, fatally struck President John F. Kennedy. Connally, who was wounded while seated directly in front of the president in the open car, insisted he was hit in the back by the sniper's second shot. He didn't hear it, he said, but he felt it.

He never accepted the so-called "magic bullet" theory propounded by Warren Commission investigators. They believed that the wounds to the governor's back, chest, wrist and thigh could have been caused by a single bullet, a bullet that had first coursed through Kennedy's body.

Consistent in his recollection of the sequence of shots, the governor was puzzled by other aspects of the Dallas tragedy. His final public comment on the ambush, published after his death on June 15, 1993, is a somber voice from the tomb:

"Here we are, I thought, 30 years later, still speculating about what did or did not happen. And no one will ever know the complete truth." His reflections appeared in his autobiography, *In History's Shadow,* written with Mickey Herskowitz, published by Hyperion and excerpted by *Time* magazine in June 1993.

"I cannot say that I think about the assassination every day, but I don't miss it by much....The long-term effects of my injuries have been mixed. I have a slight rigidity in the right wrist. I am now plagued by a pulmonary fibrosis, which results in a shortness of breath whenever I undertake any physical exertion. My doctors attribute this condition to the assassin's bullet that ripped through my lung."

The 1963 lung wound could have figured three decades later in the pulmonary causes of the 76-year-old public figure's death, adding another twist to the convoluted historical drama.

"The doctors didn't treat the wound as they would today," Herskowitz said.

"When they patched up his lung in 1963 they left a lot of scar tissue which, I understand, likely contributed to the pulmonary fibrosis.

"He always railed against the vultures who capitalized on the tragedy," the Houston celebrity biographer said. "For many years, he didn't talk much about the assassination or his wounds. President Nixon (whom Connally served as adviser and treasury secretary) told me he'd never said a word about the subject to him."

Years before, Connally had helped steer the early political career of President

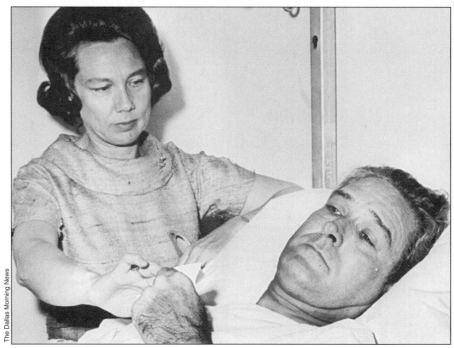

The governor is comforted by his wife, Nellie, during his recuperation at Parkland Memorial Hospital.

Lyndon B. Johnson. Connally waited a respectful period after Johnson's death, then announced his switch from the Democratic to the Republican Party. Many Texas politicos knew him as "Lyndon's boy," a tag he wore for decades.

The handsome, articulate and decorated World War II naval combat officer resigned as Kennedy's Navy secretary to run for Texas governor. He won, and served from 1963 to 1969. But before leaving Washington, he was the Navy secretary who denied turncoat Lee Harvey Oswald's request for an honorable discharge from the Marine Corps.

Denial of the request later caused speculation that the ex-Marine sought revenge by firing at Connally. A lingering but never widely accepted theory is that the sniper's real target was not JFK but JBC.

After switching parties, Connally made a disappointing bid for the Republican presidential nomination. Rebounding, he focused his energies and charm on big business deals. In Texas' 1980s economic bust, the deals soured.

"He didn't intend to write a book," said Herskowitz. "Only in recent years did he decide to tell his story. We waited more than a year after he emerged from bankruptcy to begin."

Within hours after Connally's death, JFK assassination researchers asked Attorney General Janet Reno and the FBI to help them obtain any bullet fragments that remained in the governor's body. They believed that analysis of the fragments — if any existed — might prove or disprove the conflicting assassination theories.

His widow, Nellie Connally, their three children and other kin were appalled. "The investigators had 30 years to bring up this matter," said John B. Connally III of Houston. Attuned to the family's feelings, Herskowitz said, "The request was preposterous. There'll be no exhumation. What purpose would it serve? The doctors removed the bullet fragments in 1963. There's no reason to think they overlooked any."

Those fragments removed in 1963 reportedly provided ballistic evidence

Connally and wife, Nellie, leave the plane at Dallas' Love Field. The Kennedys greet Vice President Johnson and Dallas Mayor Earle Cabell.

The Dallas Morning News

consistent with the "magic bullet" theory. That slug, well-shaped but far from pristine, was found on Connally's stretcher at Parkland. Dimensions of the entry wound in the governor's back indicated that he was hit by a tumbling bullet.

Throughout the nearly three decades of life remaining to him after that bloody November day in Dallas, Connally was never willing to accept the theory that he had shared a bullet with JFK.

ENDURING QUESTIONS

Conspiracy Theories Persist

By Bill Deener

Questions have swirled around the assassination of President John F. Kennedy for 30 years, and many conspiracy theorists now believe that the truth about the "crime of the century" may be locked away forever.

Too much time has passed, and too many witnesses have died.

And yet visitors still come to Dealey Plaza, gaze toward the sixth floor of the old Texas School Book Depository and wonder.

Was the assassination of the president the act of a lone assassin or the work of conspirators? Was the former Soviet Union or the Cuban government involved? Did members of organized crime play a role? Or the most chilling thought of all — was the FBI, CIA or LBJ behind a plot to kill the president?

The U.S. Justice Department officially ended its inquiry into the assassination in September 1988, stating that "no persuasive evidence can be identified to support the theory of a conspiracy." The Justice Department's investigation had come at the behest of the U.S. House Select Committee on Assassinations, which concluded in 1979 that Kennedy "probably" was assassinated as a result of a conspiracy involving a second gunman.

The Justice Department ruling may have convinced some that a lone gunman, Lee Harvey Oswald, shot the president, but most conspiracy theorists remained unconvinced. And their books and articles espousing one theory or another have continued unabated, slowly chipping away at the "lone gunman" theory. But it was a movie, not a book, that probably brought the notion of a conspiracy into the mainstream of American consciousness.

After the release of Oliver Stone's movie *JFK* in December 1991, many more Americans joined in the conspiracy debate.

"After that movie, it suddenly became acceptable for people to publicly discuss the fact that the president's assassination may have been the result of a conspiracy," said Jim Marrs, author of *Crossfire,* one of the books upon which the movie was based.

Stone concludes in the movie that Oswald was not the assassin. In fact, the movie implies that he wasn't even on the sixth floor of the book depository at the time of the shooting. Further, Stone believes the CIA, the Pentagon and former President Lyndon Johnson may have been involved. The film actually focuses on former New Orleans District Attorney Jim Garrison and his efforts to convict New Orleans businessman Clay Shaw of being involved in the assassination plot.

The movie was both praised as brilliant filmmaking and ridiculed as director Stone's paranoia run amok. Whatever the assessment, the movie did accomplish one thing, said Michael Kurtz, an assassination researcher and history professor at South-eastern Louisiana University in Hammond, La.

It forced Congress to pass the President John F. Kennedy Assassination Records Collection Act of 1992, which requires any federal agency holding assassination-related documents to transfer them to the National Archives. The federal government unlocked the huge cache of records August 23, 1993.

"I think Stone did a public service by really arousing public opinion to demand that the government release probably over a million pages of suppressed documents on the assassination," said Kurtz.

The first inquiry into the assassination, conducted by the Warren Commission, began only days after the president's death. The commission, after hearing testimony from 552 witnesses and reviewing thousands of pages of documents, concluded in 1964 that Oswald, acting alone, fired three shots from a sixth-floor window of the Texas School Book Depository on Elm Street.

One of the shots missed the presidential limousine. One struck Kennedy in the upper back, exited through his throat and hit Texas Gov. John Connally. Another shot hit Kennedy in the head, killing him, the commission said. The commission was unable to determine which of the three shots went awry.

The seven-member Warren Commission concluded that there was no conspiracy. According to former President Gerald

Right: A rifle-scope view during a re-enactment of the assassination in May 1964.

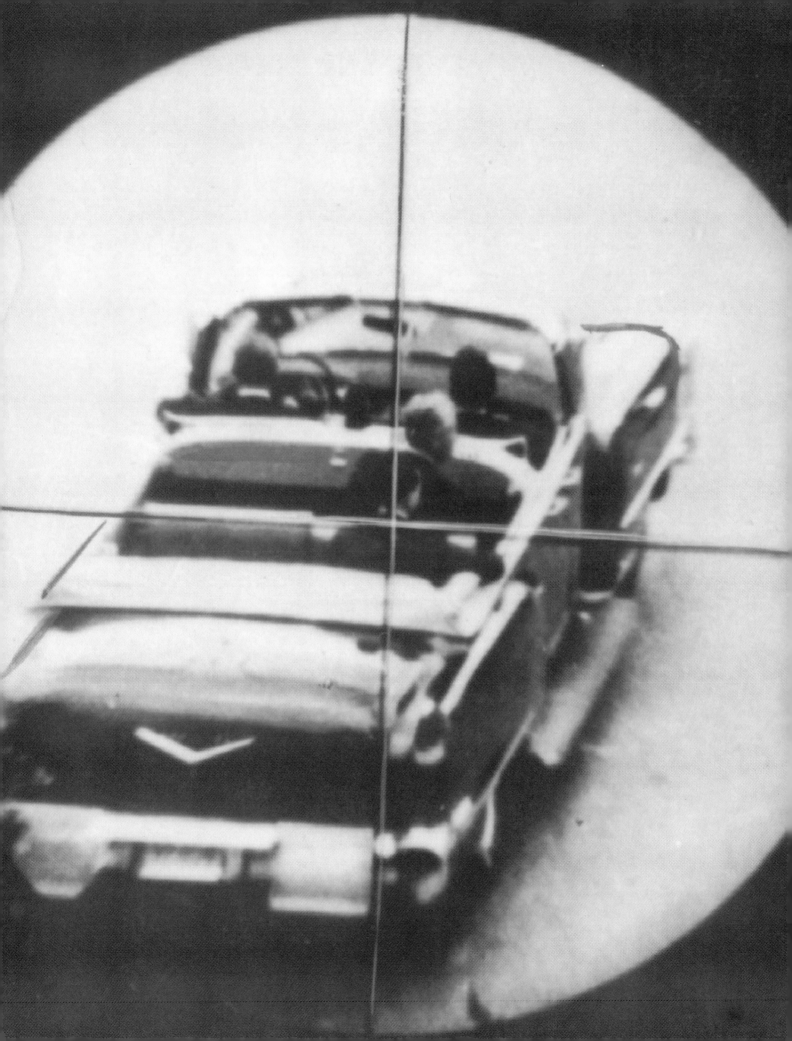

Ford, who served on the commission while a congressman, "The two basic decisions of the Warren Commission have not been successfully challenged. The Warren Commission said Lee Harvey Oswald committed the assassination. No credible evidence or theory has been produced to the contrary. The commission also stated no evidence had been found as to a conspiracy, foreign or domestic. No new facts have been disclosed that undermine that conclusion."

At first most of the public embraced the 888-page Warren report as the definitive, accurate account of the assassination.

By 1966, however, criticism of the report was growing, and various assassination theories emerged. One of the most damaging critiques of the Warren report was contained in a book that year titled *Inquest: The Warren Commission and the Establishment of Truth* by Edward Jay Epstein. Epstein conceived the book originally as his master's thesis, which he submitted as a political science student at Cornell University.

Epstein's book concluded that the commission sought a version of the assassination that was "politically expedient" rather than the truth. It was expedient, he said, for the commission to absolve the Soviets and the Cubans of blame to avert a war.

"If the explicit purpose of the commission was to ascertain and expose the facts, the implicit purpose was to protect the national interest by dispelling rumors," Epstein wrote.

He was among the first to raise some troubling and enduring questions about the assassination. Epstein's research, while not advancing specific theories, often is credited for laying the foundation upon which many theories were built.

Epstein, who now lives in New York, was the first Warren Commission critic to publish an FBI report of the assassination that was inconsistent with the U.S. Navy's autopsy report on Kennedy. The autopsy was conducted by Cmdr. James J. Humes at Bethesda Naval Hospital outside Washington, D.C., on the evening of the assassination. Two FBI

agents, James Sibert and Francis O'Neill, attended the autopsy and took notes.

The autopsy report stated that the bullet that hit Kennedy in the upper back exited at the front of his neck. But the FBI report obtained by Epstein, dated Jan. 13, 1964, stated: "Medical examination of the president's body had revealed that the bullet which entered his back had penetrated to a distance of less than a finger length."

If the FBI report was accurate, the bullet that hit Kennedy in the back could not have hit Connally, and one of the primary findings of the Warren report would be wrong. Expert analysis of film footage of the assassination shot by Dallas amateur photographer Abraham Zapruder — who died in 1970 — showed that the maximum amount of time that could have elapsed between the neck wound to Kennedy and the wounding of Connally was 1.66 seconds.

FBI testing of Oswald's rifle showed that it would have been impossible for him to have fired the bolt-action weapon that fast. For the Warren report to stand, one bullet had to have exited Kennedy's neck and then caused Connally's wounds.

Warren Commission assistant counsel Norman Redlich told an interviewer in 1965 that "to say they were hit by separate bullets is synonymous with saying that there were two assassins."

The FBI report, which contradicted Humes' autopsy report, and the Zapruder film, which showed the president knocked backward by the fatal shot to his head, contributed to early theories that a second assassin fired from in front of the president's limousine.

Mark Lane, a New York lawyer who wrote *Rush to Judgment* in 1966, argued that the president's head wounds possibly had been caused by a bullet fired from in front of the motorcade and not "behind and somewhat above" the vehicle as the Warren report had stated. Lane's book — filled with speculation — became a best seller, and Lane became an instant celebrity.

The books by Epstein and Lane —

and Josiah Thompson's *Six Seconds in Dallas,* which contended that Kennedy had been hit in a cross fire — popularized the belief that the Warren Commission had glossed over the truth.

The publication of their books was followed by a torrent of assassination theories.

The first wave, during the mid- to late 1960s, focused primarily on the physical evidence of the crime — the bullets, the wounds, the weapon. Not until the mid-1970s did the assassination literature delve into other questions — such as who, if anyone, hired Oswald.

G. Robert Blakey, the former chief counsel for the U.S. House Select Committee on Assassinations and currently a University of Notre Dame law professor, wrote in *The Plot to Kill the President,* published in 1981, that the Warren report "would have withstood the critical barrage, which by the mid-1970s had diminished to tedious nitpicking," had it not been for revelations that the CIA had tried to assassinate foreign leaders.

The Select Senate Committee to Study Governmental Operations, which was formed to examine the behavior of the CIA and FBI, uncovered numerous attempts to kill Cuban leader Fidel Castro.

The committee's interim report, published in November 1975, stated that the CIA had elicited the help of organized crime figures to have Castro killed. Richard M. Bissell, who was then the CIA's deputy director for plans, told the Senate committee that former FBI agent Robert Maheu met with Mafia bosses in August 1960 to discuss the plot to kill Castro. The report termed Maheu the CIA-Mafia "go-between."

That revelation was central to the theories of several assassination researchers who believed that Castro ordered Kennedy's assassination in retaliation for the CIA-Mafia plots against him.

Four main theories concerning who was behind the Kennedy assassination emerged during this time:

■ Kennedy was killed as a result of an international Communist plot directed by either the Kremlin or the Cuban government. Soviet leaders had boasted often that they would destroy America, and, as noted, Castro had known about CIA-Mafia plots to have him assassinated.

■ Cuban exiles living in the United States hired Oswald to kill Kennedy because the president had not crushed the Castro regime. In addition, the theory goes, the exiles blamed Kennedy for their failure to retake Cuba during the bungled Bay of Pigs invasion.

■ Organized crime was behind the assassination. The Kennedy administration had launched a fierce attack on the Mafia to try to break its grip on the Teamsters union and American life in general. Also, Kennedy had pushed to

have reputed New Orleans Mafia boss Carlos Marcello deported.

■ American intelligence agencies, most likely the CIA, had the president assassinated because he was taking a soft line on communism and was about to reorganize the agency. He wanted to make it more responsive to the president's office after the failure of the Bay of Pigs invasion, the theorists say. Such a reorganization would have usurped some of the CIA's autonomy and power.

Historian Kurtz of Southeastern Louisiana University, is one supporter of the theory that Castro, or pro-Castro factions in the United States, had the president killed.

"Castro was aware of the plots against him, plots concocted with the CIA's approval. Castro also knew that militant anti-Castro exile organizations based in the United States were continuing to launch raids against Cuba," Kurtz writes in *Crime of the Century.*

Kurtz said that two events suggest Cuban involvement. First, on Sept. 17, 1963, a Cuban informant for the CIA, code-named "D," told the agency he saw Oswald receive a payoff at the Cuban consulate in Mexico City. The money changed hands after assassinating Kennedy was discussed, the informant said. Second, Kurtz said, the CIA learned about four months after the assassination

Associated Press

In 1964, Chief Justice Earl Warren presents the official report on the assassination to President Johnson. At left, Rep. Gerald Ford.

Associated Press

Books by Mark Lane and Edward Jay Epstein (pictured to the right) popularized the notion that the Warren Commission glossed over the truth.

that a Cuban-American implicated in the assassination "crossed the border from Texas to Mexico on 23 November, stayed in Mexico for four days, and flew to Cuba on 27 November."

Kurtz also theorized that anti-Castro factions may have used Oswald as a "patsy," hiring Oswald, an avowed communist, to kill the president, knowing that his communist ties would divert blame from the exiles. Kurtz cited some testimony before the House Select Committee on Assassinations in 1979 as evidence.

In September 1963, two Cubans and an American identified as "Leon Oswald" visited the Dallas apartment of Silvia and Annie Odio, who, according to their testimony, supported the Cuban exile cause.

One of the Cubans, named Leopoldo, told the two sisters that he supported the exiles' cause and needed their help to raise money. The meeting was brief, and Leon

Oswald said little. But two days later, Leopoldo telephoned Silvia Odio.

She quoted Leopoldo as saying of Leon Oswald: "He's an ex-Marine, and an expert marksman. He would be a tremendous asset to anyone, except that you never know how to take him. He's kind of loco, kind of nuts. He could go either way. He could do anything — like getting underground in Cuba, like killing Castro. The American says we should have shot President Kennedy after the Bay of Pigs."

After Kennedy was assassinated, Silvia Odio told authorities that Lee Harvey Oswald was the man she had known as Leon Oswald.

Probably one of the most reputable groups to establish a conspiracy theory was the U.S. House Select Committee on Assassinations. In its final report, dated March 29, 1979, the summary states: "President John F. Kennedy was probably assassinated as a result of a conspiracy."

At the heart of the theory was the committee's finding that four shots, not three, were fired at the presidential motorcade, though the National Academy of Sciences later disputed the House committee's research.

The House committee report states: "With a certainty factor of 95 percent or better, there was a shot fired at the presidential limousine from the grassy knoll."

This percentage was established by expert acoustical analysis of the original Dictabelt recordings of the Dallas Police Department transmissions made on Channel One the day of the assassination.

Committee investigators obtained the tapes from officer Paul McCaghren, who had taken possession of them in 1969 after then-Police Chief Frank Dyson found them in a locked cabinet outside his office.

The sound impulses on the tapes from Nov. 22, 1963, were compared with impulses taken during a recreation of the assassination near the intersection of Houston and Elm streets on Aug. 20, 1978. The report by the committee — which spent $5 million to study the assassinations of Kennedy and Martin Luther King — was praised by critics of the

The Dallas Morning News

Edward Jay Epstein

Warren Commission report as vindication of their years of work.

But the National Academy of Sciences, in a 1982 study of the same acoustical data, concluded that the House committee's report was incorrect.

"The acoustic analyses do not demonstrate that there was a grassy knoll shot," the academy report stated, "and in particular there is no acoustic basis for the claim of a 95 percent probability of such a shot."

The sounds analyzed by the House committee were recorded about one minute after the assassination, the report said. The academy identified some "cross talk" from Channel Two recorded on Channel One that could not have been recorded during the assassination.

The theory that members of the Mafia may have been involved in Kennedy's slaying also arose during the committee's hearings.

Although organized crime as a group was not involved, the report said, "the available evidence does not preclude the possibility that individual members may have been involved."

Blakey, the former chief counsel for the House committee, later expanded on the theory at which the committee had only hinted in his book *The Plot to Kill the President.* In this book and in its updated version, *Fatal Hour,* published in 1992, Blakey implicates organized crime figures in the assassination.

He pointed to Jack Ruby's ties to the Mafia as well as to Oswald's less-direct links to organized crime.

"Explain Jack Ruby. If he was acting on his own it was a psychological problem, but it's clear it wasn't a psychological problem. The more reasonable explanation is that it was motivated as a group and that group is the mob," Blakey said during an interview in 1988.

Blakey surveyed in minute detail Ruby's ties to the Mafia: He had been personally acquainted with two professional killers for the crime syndicate, David Yaras and Lenny Patrick; among Ruby's closest friends was Lewis McWillie, who, Blakey said, had ties to Florida Mafia don Santo Trafficante.

McWillie operated casinos in Havana from 1958 until 1960, and Ruby visited him in August 1959, according to Ruby's testimony before the Warren Commission. But Blakey said that Ruby lied about the number of trips he made to Cuba.

"We came to believe that Ruby's trips to Cuba, were, in fact, organized-crime activities," Blakey said. "We concluded, in short, that Ruby consciously set out to kill Oswald, that he stalked him and shot him with no apparent motive other than to silence him."

Blakey connected Oswald to organized crime primarily through two men. The first was Oswald's uncle, Charles F. Murret, who had a long history of bookmaking and gambling activities. The key point, though, was that Murret subscribed to a "Marcello-controlled wire service, an illegal means for bookmakers to obtain race results. As such, he (Murret) had made regular payments to Marcello."

Blakey places special importance on Oswald's having known David Ferrie, whom Blakey called "an operative for Carlos Marcello in 1963." Oswald met Ferrie in the mid-1950s when both served in a Civil Air Patrol unit in New Orleans.

Blakey suggested that the Mafia's motive to kill Kennedy was that it feared his administration would destroy it through stepped-up prosecution. Members of organized crime hired Ruby to kill Oswald so the conspiracy would not be revealed, he said.

The remains of Lee Harvey Oswald were exhumed in 1981 after it was theorized that an impostor was buried in his grave as part of a Soviet plot.

Blakey gave the Mafia the motive and the means but did not offer direct evidence that organized crime was involved until he updated *The Plot to Kill the President* in 1992. This version, *Fatal Hour,* contains what purports to be the deathbed confession of Trafficante to Frank Ragano, a lawyer who worked for organized crime figures.

In 1986, as Trafficante, 72, lay dying in a Houston hospital, he summoned the trusted counselor Ragano to his bedside. Ragano quoted Trafficante as saying: "We should not have killed Giovanni (John). We should have killed Bobby (former Attorney General Robert Kennedy)."

Blakey said in a July 1993 interview, "I believe there probably was a conspiracy, and if there was, the mob was involved."

The chief proponent of the theory that American intelligence officers were involved in the assassination is British journalist Anthony Summers. He believes that anti-Castro factions, helped by the CIA, persuaded Oswald to kill Kennedy.

"It is certainly possible that a renegade element in U.S. intelligence manipulated Oswald — whatever his role on Nov. 22, 1963. That same element may have activated pawns in the anti-Castro movement and the Mafia to murder the president and to execute Oswald," Summers wrote in his book *Conspiracy,* published in 1980.

Summers said renegade members of the CIA, passionately opposed to Castro,

tried to sabotage the president's desire to reconcile relations with Cuba.

They sponsored "unauthorized raids on Soviet shipping after the missile crisis," Summers said.

One CIA agent assembled Cuban exiles in Guatemala before the Bay of Pigs invasion, Summers said, and told them that "there were forces in the administration trying to block the invasion."

The agent said that if the order came, they were to ignore it and proceed with the Cuban invasion, according to Summers. "While the Assassinations Committee rightly concluded that the CIA as an agency had no part in the assassination, it is wholly possible that mavericks from the intelligence world were involved," Summers said.

Not surprising, over the past three decades assassination researchers have produced many other theories, and what they lacked in plausibility they made up for in creativity. A man carrying an umbrella, one theory says, fired small rockets at the president. Researcher David Lifton, author of *Best Evidence,* contends in his book that Kennedy's body was altered before the autopsy to make entrance wounds appear to be exit wounds.

In 1981, conspiracy theories took a bizarre turn when Michael H.B. Eddowes, a 91-year-old British researcher, instigated the exhumation of the remains of Lee Harvey Oswald.

Eddowes, who suggested there had been a Soviet plot to kill Kennedy, believed an impostor was buried in the grave. But medical tests confirmed that the body was Oswald's.

While books on the assassination now number in the hundreds, one of the more unique offerings in this the 30th year since the assassination is probably Robert J. Groden's *The Killing of a President: The Complete Photographic Record of the JFK Assassination, the Conspiracy and the Cover-Up.* Mr. Groden, of Boothwyn, Pa., the former staff photographic consultant to the House Select Committee on Assassinations, collected more than 600 photographs relating to the assassination.

Using computer-enhanced photographs, Mr. Groden says that the evidence shows the shots that killed the president came from the front, not the rear, and that this proves there was a conspiracy. But Mr. Groden makes no claims about who may have killed the president.

He probably summed up the sentiments of many researchers when he said, "The more you investigate it, the farther away you seem to get."

Former staff writer William J. Choyke contributed to this report. The article, written for The News' *1983 special report on the Kennedy assassination, was updated in 1993.*

THE TEXAS SCHOOL BOOK DEPOSITORY

A Tribute to the Life and Death of JFK

By Shermakaye Bass

The elevator descends six floors of the old Texas School Book Depository.

Its riders are pensive as they reflect on what they have just seen. They talk of conspiracies, legacies, sadness and release.

They talk about the sensation of standing in a place where history's course was dramatically recharted.

They have just visited the Sixth Floor, a tribute to the life and death of John F. Kennedy.

During their tour of the exhibit, the visitors have stood on the same floor that Lee Harvey Oswald trod. They have seen the same view of Dealey Plaza and Elm Street as it curved toward the triple underpass. The experience has been an emotional one.

Each person has paused at the sniper's perch. The corner area is encased in glass now. An eerie stillness envelopes stacks of book boxes arranged as they might have been on Nov. 22, 1963.

Many have watched the historic broadcast in which Walter Cronkite announced to the nation that the president was dead. They have examined the Zapruder frames showing Kennedy's last moments. They have listened to his words as he launched his presidency:

"We stand today on the edge of a new frontier...a frontier of unknown opportunities and paths, a frontier of unfulfilled hopes and threats."

What the visitors have seen at the Sixth Floor exhibit is John Kennedy himself — his life and death captured in a moving display of still images, video, text and audio.

Organized and maintained by the Dallas County Historical Foundation, the exhibit draws between 1,200 and 2,500 tourists each day. It is a comprehensive, chronologically ordered look at the events surrounding Kennedy's administration, his assassination and its aftermath.

The exhibit is educational: Dozens of texts and images recount the assassination; panels present acoustical, forensic and ballistic evidence and explore the federal investigations into Kennedy's death. Its effect, though, is unmistakably emotional.

Panels at the Sixth Floor exhibit recount the events and evidence surrounding the assassination.

A visitor looks down from the sixth floor of the Texas School Book Depository over the grassy knoll where Kennedy was slain.

The Dallas Morning News

"It kind of allows you to grieve," says Bob Porter, director of public programs for the foundation, which was instituted specifically for the exhibit's creation.

Many people have come to Dallas seeking closure, he says, and by revisiting the site, they often find it.

Their responses are documented in the "Memory Books" just outside the sixth floor elevator. The books contain notes in many languages — Spanish, Japanese, French, Swedish and English. There are notes from young children, from adults who hadn't been born when Kennedy was assassinated, and from those who remember the event all too vividly.

One British tourist wrote in the logs: "After 30 years of wondering where and what the 'killing' scene was like, I return to England with renewed thoughts and shall always remember that day."

The three-and-a-half-year-old museum provides a contrast to the Kennedy Memorial, Philip Johnson's cenotaph at the corner of Commerce and Main streets. For years, the empty granite enclosure was the only site for public mourning, and those who traveled to Dallas to pay homage often left feeling their mission was incomplete.

"Hundreds of thousands of people were in Dallas every year, and they were walking around Dealey Plaza looking for something — information and understanding," Mr. Porter says. "That was the motivating factor for this museum."

Since it opened in the former school book depository, now the Dallas County Administration Building, nearly 1.35 million people have passed through its doors.

Wearing cameras and walking shoes, pushing baby strollers or walkers, many find themselves completely absorbed in the exhibit's segments: The Early '60s, The Trip to Texas, The Corner Window, Views Into Dealey Plaza, The Crisis Hours, The Investigations, Who Did It?, The Legacy, and The Corner Staircase.

The area labeled "The Crisis Hours" is perhaps the most moving. Here is where visitors relive the moments and days following Kennedy's assassination. In a dark, partitioned area, a large projector screen shows footage from Kennedy's funeral — the moment when Mrs. Kennedy and Caroline knelt at the president's coffin to kiss the American flag, the instant when John-John saluted the riderless horse as the funeral procession passed.

In this area, a young mother puts her arm around her son. "This really happened," she tells the boy. "It's really sad."

Like everyone who comes to the Sixth Floor, they will leave with an indelible impression of John Kennedy, the youngest president in American history. They will know how the world mourned, and they will pass, on their way out, a large black and white photo of carnations left at the Kennedy Memorial 10 years ago. Attached to the flowers is a note: "Here passed a man. With hope, we chose to follow, one brief shining moment."